CLINTON TOWNSHIP PUBLIC LIB
P9-DNY-900
Storage

Czech Republic

HUBERTUS

Czech Republic

BY JOANN MILIVOJEVIC

Enchantment of the World
Second Series

Children's Press®
A Division of Scholastic Inc.
NEW YORK TORONTO LONDON AUCKLAND SYDNEY
MEXICO CITY NEW DELHI HONG KONG
DANBURY, CONNECTICUT

Frontispiece: East Bohemia winter

Consultant: Hana Pichova, Department of Slavic Languages and Literatures,
The University of Texas at Austin

Please note: All statistics are as up-to-date as possible at the time of publication.

Book production by Herman Adler Design

Library of Congress Cataloging-in-Publication Data

Milivojevic, JoAnn.
Czech Republic / by JoAnn Milivojevic.
p. cm. — (Enchantment of the World. Second series)
Includes bibliographical references and index.
ISBN 0-516-24255-5
1. Czech Republic—Juvenile literature. [1. Czech Republic.] I. Title. II. Series.
DB2065.M55 2003
943.71—dc21 2003011129

1 2 3 4 5 6 7 8 9 10 R 13 12 11 10 09 08 07 06 05 04

Czech Republic

Contents

CHAPTER

Cover photo:
Vltava River,
Prague

Czech countryside

Folk musicians

The Heart of Europe

The Czech Republic has been referred to as the heart of Europe because it sits in the center of the European landmass. Bohemia is the largest region of what is now called the Czech Republic. This central geographic position has been both a blessing and a curse. It is a blessing because the country's central location has made it a desirable place to live but this can be a curse because many people have wanted to conquer it. Since Bohemia began to emerge as a distinct culture around the tenth century, surrounding conquerors sought this land and its people. Historically, neighbors such as Germany and Austria (i.e., the Austro-Hungarian Empire) waged war. But in later years, Soviet Communists nearly squeezed the cultural life out of this fascinating region. Today, those quarrels are nearly forgotten or, as Czech graffiti artists suggest, ought to be completely forgotten. Their scribblings around the capital city of Prague reflect that attitude with slogans such as "destroy the past, live for the future."

Opposite: **The Czech Republic is a country located in Central Europe.**

Young graffiti artists spray paint a cement wall in Prague.

To forget the Czech past would mean to say goodbye to an incredible history filled with enviable accomplishments. Amazing castles, talented artists, and clever statesmen would disappear from memory. Fortunately, the accomplishments of the Czechs will endure because neither the Czech government, educators, nor the world at large will allow the past to be erased. Many Czech monuments and entire Czech towns are memorialized on the World Heritage List, an organization that preserves historical and cultural entities of international importance. In this way, a culture survives and can build its future upon a strong foundation.

In recent history, the Czechs have been celebrated for their passive resistance. Rather than violence, they have chosen a path of peaceful protest. By rallying in the streets in massive numbers, they successfully threw off the handcuffs of Communism. They are a perfect example of what citizens united against a cause can accomplish. Czechs believed they deserved to be a free and independent country. Through their peaceful persistence they won their independence.

Art and Education: The Heart of the Czech Nation

Historically, the Czechs have spent most of their years under foreign rule. They have had, however, some periods of independence. In 1918, the Czechs united with their neighbors, the Slovaks, to create a country called Czechoslovakia. But even as a country united with its neighbor, Czechoslovakia was subject to foreign rulers. Many of its years were spent as a Communist country with the Soviet Union controlling most

of its activities. The Czech Republic and Slovakia remained joined until 1993. Today, the Czech Republic is an independent democratic country.

Historical reenactments are a popular form of live entertainment throughout the Republic.

In some ways, the Czech Republic is like a child just learning to stand on its own. Unlike a naive child, it is supported by centuries of achievement, especially in education and the arts. The Czech people have long been recognized for their artistic and intellectual abilities. From poets, playwrights, painters, and puppeteers to architects, musicians, and writers, the art world has often looked to the Czechs for what is hot and happening. For example, in the fourteenth century, the Czechs developed a unique style of architecture that became known as Vladislav Gothic. This style can still be seen in the capital city of Prague; the astrological clock in the city's square is a notable example. At one time, Prague was second only to Paris as a cutting-edge city for the arts. Musicians and composers such as Bedřich Smetana, known as the father of Bohemian national music, became popular on a worldwide scale. Symphony orchestras continue to play his compositions today. Václav Havel, a writer, became the Czech Republic's first president.

McDonald's makes its mark on Gothic architecture in Prague.

Fine artists don't develop without a good education. The Czechs were among the first in Europe to establish universities and schools dedicated to the arts. The Academy of the Fine Arts in Prague opened in 1796. It is the oldest art education institution in the Czech Republic. Students today earn master's and doctoral degrees in many artistic fields such as news media, painting, sculpture, and restoration of art works.

Dramatic events, foreign occupiers, periods of decline, and times of great abundance have all shaped the Czech Republic. Prague has been

called the city of a hundred spires, magic city, and golden city. Regardless of the name, it has sparked the curiosity of many. Today, Prague is one of the most visited cities in central Europe. Visitors can see its history come to life in the well-preserved architecture while at the same time eating at the fast food restaurants that have entered virtually every city on the planet. Every country is influenced and influences its neighbors, and the Czech Republic is no exception. It is a country to be admired through its love of art, rejection of armed conflict, and passion for education.

CHAPTER

TWO

Framed by Mountains

Opposite: **The Pravčická Gate is a famous natural stone bridge.**

THE CZECH REPUBLIC IS SHAPED LIKE A FREE-FORM RECTangle with mountains framing its edges. Because they make logical natural dividers, geographical formations such as rivers and mountains are often boundaries between countries.

Beyond the mountains of the Czech Republic, bordering countries include Poland to the northeast, Slovakia to the southeast, Austria to the southwest, and Germany to the west and north. Dividing them are mountains. These rising rocky beauties not only serve as natural borders, they influence weather, life, and lifestyles in the Czech Republic.

The mountains in the Czech Republic come in many shapes, sizes, and mineral compositions. Like mountains elsewhere, they were formed millions of years ago when plates deep below the surface of the earth pushed into each other and forced the land above to fold and rise. Volcanic eruptions, rain, snow, and wind further formed the mountains and the surrounding landscapes. There are no active volcanoes in the Czech Republic today, but hot volcanic rock lies deep beneath the surface. These hot rocks serve an important purpose. They heat water that has seeped down into the earth, creating hot springs. Hot springs in the Czech Republic are used for natural healing.

The area of the Czech Republic is 30,450 square miles (78,864 square kilometers). It is 305 miles east to west (490 kilometers) and about 175 miles (280 km) north to south.

Bohemia is the largest region in the Czech Republic.

The country is split into two main regions: the western portion, Bohemia, covers about two-thirds of the territory; to the east is Moravia. The regions are divided by the Bohemian-Moravian highlands, a small hilly area.

Bohemia is basically a plateau surrounded by low mountains, rolling hills, and valleys. Moravia sits on hilly lowlands with patches of flat fertile land, perfect for farming. Within northeastern Moravia is a sliver of land called Silesia. It borders on Poland and was once a part of Poland. Today, Silesia is remembered for its unique cultural and historic characteristics.

The Province of Bohemia

Bohemia is divided into five regions: north, south, central, east, and west. The mountains of northern Bohemia have been heavily mined for ore and coal. The factories here have spewed out tons of waste, making the northern region the most polluted area in the Czech Republic.

Get up high into the northern mountains, however, and you'll be surrounded by natural beauty. Northern Bohemia is home to the Czech Republic's highest mountain peak, Sněžka (SNUH-ez-kah), meaning snow, which rises to 5,256 feet (1,602 meters). It is part of the Krkonoše (Giant) mountain range that borders Poland and Germany.

The giant Krkonoše Mountain range borders Poland.

Mountain Legend

Once upon a time, a long-bearded, pipe-smoking man named Krkonoš lived high atop the windswept Krkonoše Mountains. He was the ruler of those mountains and had magical powers. He could use his powers for good or evil. Mostly, he used them to change the weather. For example, imagine enjoying a picnic on a beautiful and sunny afternoon. The birds are singing and the breeze is warm. There's not a cloud in the sky. Then suddenly, Krkonoš blasts a flurry of hail down upon the land, sending you running for cover. Within a few minutes, the sunny weather is back. You return to a sopping wet picnic basket wondering what happened. People say the legend of Krkonoš developed as a way to explain the sudden shifts in weather that occur in this area.

But this ruler of the Krkonoše Mountains doesn't just belong to Czech legend. Many people of German descent have also lived in this area. Germans called this mountain master Ruebezahl. The name means, "he who counts turnips." But it wasn't he that was doing all the counting. It is said that he got lonely and so he kidnapped a princess. To keep her from escaping while he was busy playing with the weather, he made her count his turnips.

Head to the southwest region of Bohemia and you'll find the Šumava Forest, an area thick with fir trees such as spruce and pine. Nature lovers adore this region because it is in pristine

The Šumava Forest is especially popular with nature lovers.

natural condition. Very little of this land has been farmed or industrialized with factories. Here you will find sparkling glacial lakes, large ponds, and soggy peat bogs. The ponds are both natural and man-made. The oldest and largest artificial pond, dug out in 1590, is Rožmberk near Treboň. Natural and man-made ponds are both beautiful and functional. Many are used to raise carp, a type of freshwater fish that loves shallow muddy bottoms. Carp is harvested from these ponds and enjoyed by Czechs, especially during Christmas.

Peat Bogs

Peat is a dark, rich organic matter. It grows in watery areas with poor drainage. In the stagnant water, organisms grow among decaying plants. The organisms bind together and form a spongy muck, called peat, which is very high in carbon. Peat is the first step in the formation of coal. Some peat bogs in Bohemia have been turned into tourist attractions. Wooden walkways built over the bogs allow visitors to check out the landscape. Without the walkways, you'd sink right into the bog.

Boubin Virgin Forest

The southern Bohemian mountain range has some of the oldest virgin forest in the world. In 1838, a nobleman decided that the area must remain natural and forbade anyone to use it for commercial purposes. Today, it is still a protected nature reserve. Because the wildlife and plants have not been disturbed by humans, it is considered among the most beautiful areas of the Czech Republic. It is here where you can see giant trees such as a 460-year-old spruce that stands 189 feet (57.5 m) high.

Both the northern and southern mountain regions are popular with people who enjoy outdoor activities. In winter, snow covers the higher parts of the mountains, making them perfect for skiing. In the north, major international ski jumping championships are held in Harachov (in the Krkonoše Mountains) every year. In the south during the summer, cyclists take to the hills for a challenging race to determine the King of Šumava Mountain.

In the highlands of central Bohemia there is an interesting natural rock formation called karst. Karst is porous, thick limestone. Through millions of years, water has dissolved and worn away different parts of the limestone, leaving behind a large system of caves and underground rivers. The area with the most caves is just south of Prague. Named the Koneprusy Caves, the system is more than 230 feet (70 m) deep and more than a mile (2 km) long. There are three layers of passages. Parts of the cave are open to the public.

Water has worn down limestone inside karst caves leaving behind dramatic formations.

Healing Waters

The west side of Bohemia is rich in natural spring waters, both hot and cold. Because of this, many health spas have been built in the area. The waters are said to cure digestive, heart, circulatory, and other health problems. People bathe in or drink various waters from the region depending on what ails them. The most famous spa town, Karlovy Vary (KAR-lohv-VEE VAR-ree), meaning Charles Spa, named after King Charles IV, has been operating since the 1500s. Today, more than 2 million people from around the world visit every year. Some come to see the incredible architecture while others take advantage of the many spa cures.

There are twelve different kinds of springs in Karlovy Vary, each with a different temperature and mineral content. The hottest spring is a scalding 160° Fahrenheit (70° Celsius). How do you know which spring is right for you? Doctors at the spa prescribe specific therapies and mineral springs. Some waters, however, can be freely consumed from one of the many flowing fountains. The waters vary in taste, some have a heavy metallic flavor and can only be consumed in small sips. Special cups have been developed making it easier to drink just a little bit of water at a time.

Drinking the waters and taking baths are the most common therapies. But there are some rather unusual therapies in

People drink mineral water from a fountain in Karlovy Vary, a famous spa town.

Karlovy Vary, among them the dry carbon dioxide bath and the Peloid wrap. The dry bath involves sealing a patient's body inside a plastic bag, then filling the bag with carbon dioxide. Patients absorb the gas through the skin. The therapy is said to heal wounds and lower blood pressure. The Peloid wrap uses hot water mixed with peat moss pulled from Bohemian bogs. The warm mixture is smeared on the area of the body that needs to be healed.

Sandstone Sculpture

Česky ráj (CHESS-kee rahzh), meaning Bohemian paradise, in eastern Bohemia is most notable for its dramatic sandstone landscape. Through the years, rain has cut deep gorges into the rocks, leaving behind tall sculpted spires. There are so many sandstone clusters that the Czechs labeled some of them as Rock Towns. The most popular is Hruba Skala, which has hundreds of sandstone pillars, some reaching as high as 1,200 feet (380 m). Hiking and rock climbing are extremely popular sports here.

In addition to rocks for climbing, Česky ráj is also well known for its many semiprecious stones. The rocky landscape is littered with agate, jasmine, and chalcedony—all in the quartz family. Garnet, a beautiful red gemstone, is also found here. Skilled artists cut and polish these stones for use in jewelry.

Hruba Skala attracts sightseers and rock climbers.

Looking at the Czech Republic's Cities

Established in 1243 is the city of Brno (above). With a population of 388,596, it is the second largest city in the Czech Republic. It is surrounded by pretty countryside and rolling hills. Brno's lowest point is 620 feet (190 m) and its highest elevation is 1,395 feet (425 m) above sea level. Brno is located in Moravia, which is the cradle of Czech civilization and where the Great Moravian Empire began. The city has many famous historic buildings including the Noble Women's palace, which was dedicated to caring for the orphaned daughters of noblemen.

Pilsen (Plzeň), population 171,908, was established as a town by Czech king Wenceslas II in 1295. It is located where four rivers meet, making it an important center of trade in its early days. Pilsen, at 1,010 feet (307 m) above sea level, is in western Bohemia and is the fourth largest city in the country. It is best known for its beer, Pilsner Urquell. It is the world's first pilsner beer, a light, refreshing beverage that is cherished by beer lovers around the world. The city's brewery was founded in 1842 and the original Gothic building is still used to brew beer. The city is also home to the Skoda manufacturing company, which makes autos and heavy machinery.

Turnov was founded in the thirteenth century and is located near the Jizera River. The town is famous for its jewelry artisans and has a school dedicated to jewelry-making. When the School of Applied Arts opened its doors back in 1884, it was the first school of its kind in Europe. Trade and crafts were the primary industries during the town's early years. Today, 14,600 people live in the town and most work in tourism or the jewelry industry.

The Province of Moravia

On the eastern side of the Czech Republic is Moravia. Like Bohemia, there are areas suited to farming, outdoor sports, and tourism. The mountain regions include Jeseníky, the highest range in Moravia. The area is popular for summer and winter sports such as downhill skiing and hiking.

The southern portion of Moravia consists of gently rolling hills with soil ideal for growing grapes. There are many large vineyards throughout southern Moravia. Brno is the main city and the second largest in the Czech Republic. Near Brno is another karst area famous for its caves. The Moravský Kras (MO-rav-skee Krahs), or Moravian Karst, caves have some amazing formations of stalactites and stalagmites. Stalactites hang like icicles from the roofs of caves, whereas stalagmites form on cave floors. The Punkva, an underground river, flows through these caves. Tour boats float on this underground river allowing visitors to see the magnificent caves.

Farms dot the Moravian countryside.

The Bílé Karpaty (BEY-lee KAR-pity), or White Carpathian Mountains, separate Moravia and Slovakia. The mountains have a white appearance because they are composed of quartz and mica. The many meadows of colorful wildflowers make the hillsides of the White Carpathians an especially beautiful place to visit in the springtime.

Rivers and Lakes

The Czech Republic may be landlocked but is it home to many water sources. In addition to rivers, there are 455 natural lakes and 21,800 artificial lakes and ponds. Most of the man-made ponds are used as fish farms.

Three main rivers in the Czech Republic provide an outlet to the sea. The rivers in southern Moravia join with the Danube River, which flows to the Black Sea, the Labe River eventually extends to the North Sea, and the Oder River reaches the Baltic Sea. The Vltava, the Republic's national

The Vltava River flows near the Rožmberk Castle.

Worst Flood in 100 Years

In August 2002, huge rains caused the Vltava River to flood. More than 200,000 people were forced from their homes. The raging water and debris destroyed railway bridges, flooded train stations, and knocked out phone and electrical lines. Damage was estimated to be in the millions of dollars. Fortunately, most historical monuments were spared, notably the Charles Bridge in Prague, which stretches over the Vltava.

The last major flood was in 1890. The Vltava rose more that 6 feet (2 m). That time the Charles Bridge was not so lucky. Three arches were torn away and two statues were swallowed by the river. It took fourteen years to repair the damage.

river, is a branch, or tributary, of the Labe (Elbe) River. The Vltava's source is high up in the Šumava mountain range in southern Bohemia. It is the longest river in the Republic, flowing 270 miles (435 km). The Vltava is an important source of hydroelectric power.

Environmental Conservation

During the forty years of Communist rule, from 1948 to1989, care of the natural environment was not a top concern. Industrial contamination from heavy metal factories and agricultural waste seeped into the soil and polluted the sky. These pollutants created serious problems in many parts of the Czech Republic, especially in the northern regions. Since the Czech Republic became independent in 1993, the new government has taken serious steps to protect the environment. Several mines have been closed, tighter pollution controls have been established, and many areas have been declared as nature reserves.

The Czech Republic has four sanctioned national parks; Krkonoše (the first to be established in 1963), Šumava, Podyjí, and České Švýcarsko (above). In addition, there are many protected nature reserves. Most of these government-protected areas are open to visitors and are free of charge.

Climate

The climate in the Czech Republic is continental, meaning cold winters and warm summers. There are four distinct seasons:

summer, autumn, winter, spring. The hottest month is July. The coldest is January. The mountains get the most snow and some may even have snow cover through May. Due to warmer winds that blow from the southwest, Bohemia is a bit milder in temperature than Moravia. Countrywide, the average temperature in winter is 22°F (–5°C) and in summer it's a pleasant 68°F (20°C). It rains more in the summer than during other seasons.

The Czech Republic's Geographical Features

Highest Point: Sněžka Mountain, 5,256 feet (1,602 m)
Lowest Point: Labe River, 384 feet (117 m)
Coldest Point: Sněžka Mountain
Longest River: Vltava, 270 miles (435 km)
Oldest and Largest Artificial Pond: Rožmberk, south Bohemia, 1,235 acres (500 ha)
Largest City: Prague, 1.2 million people
Oldest Primeval Forest: Boubin Virgin Forest, south Bohemia
Area with the Most Natural Springs: Western Bohemia
Longest Natural Stone Bridge: Pravčická Gate, Northern Bohemia, spans 89 feet (27 m)
Deepest Gorge: Hranice gorge, central Moravia, 800 feet (244 m)
Average Temperatures: Prague, January, 27°F (–3°C); July, 64°F (18°C); Brno, January, 29°F (–2°C); July, 67°F (19°C)
Precipitation: Prague, 18.8 inches (477 mm); Brno, 19.6 inches (497 mm)

CHAPTER THREE

Plants and Animals

The Czech Republic is similar in size to the U.S. state of South Carolina. Quite a lot of wildlife is packed into this small space. The many mountains, hills, valleys, rivers, and ponds provide various habitats for a large variety of plant and animal life. Add to that what farmers raise, and you'll find a country rich in wildlife diversity.

Opposite: **Forests in the Czech Republic are home to many animals.**

Before we take a look at what crawls, tweets, and sprouts around the country today, let's glimpse back in time. About 1.8 million years ago, during the Stone Age (also called the Paleolithic age), this region alternated between glacial and interglacial periods. The weather, terrain, and creatures that existed during these two periods were quite different. The glacial periods, as the name implies, were times of icy arctic coldness. Wooly mammoth, reindeer, and arctic fox romped the tundra. The interglacial periods were times of subtropical warmth with zebras, elephants, and rhinoceros tromping about the land. Of course, you won't find these creatures in the Czech Republic now, unless you visit the Prague Zoo.

Keeping Count

Imagine counting all the different trees, bushes, flowers, birds, animals, and insects in your neighborhood. Now do that over the entire countryside. Czech scientists have counted all the flora and fauna to gain a better understanding of their ecology. Scientists estimate that there are 369 vertebrate species (creatures with spines), 48,000 invertebrate species (including insects), 2,520 vascular plants (those with roots, stems, and leaves), and more than 848 different kinds of moss.

Česky Ráj has many rapeseed fields.

Grapes grown in vineyards are used to make wine.

Today, you'll find many of the same plants and animals that live in the midwestern United States.

Fruits, Flowers, and Farms

Agricultural crops grow best in the valleys of the Vltava and Labe Rivers and in the fertile eastern lowlands of Moravia. Farmers plant a wide variety of crops. You'll find grapevines in many regions, especially along the sunny hillsides of Moravia. In the Bohemian countryside, pretty fields of barley and hops are grown. These grains are very important because they are used to make beer, a major industry in the Czech Republic. Farmers also grow sugar beets, wheat, rapeseed, and potatoes. Sugar beets in particular have been an important export product for the

From Beets to Sugar

The fertile Morava Valley is home to many crops, including beets. Thirty percent of the world's sugar supply comes from the sugar beet. Beets are small vegetables like potatoes. They grow underground and are harvested in the fall. Who would think that sugar could be found inside such a plain-looking vegetable? But don't bite down on a beet expecting it to be sweet! To extract the sugar from the white root, beets must be heavily processed. They are washed, peeled, and chopped. Sugar is squeezed from the juice of beet parts. The dry pulp that remains is fed to animals.

Czech Republic. Sugar beets grow underground like potatoes. The large green leaves above ground capture the sun and rain to feed the plant below ground. Sugar beets are used to make sugar. In addition to crops, farmers also tend livestock such as cattle, poultry, pigs, and sheep.

A dog helps his master harvest apples.

There are lots of natural sweets to eat in the Czech Republic. Among the most popular orchard fruits are apple, plum, cherry, and pear. The fruits are enjoyed fresh, baked in tarts and pies, and are also used to make special brandies. Smaller summer fruits such as strawberries, blueberries, and currants appear in patches large and small across the Czech Republic.

A beautiful summer meadow.

Fields and Meadows

Summer is the time of flowers both cultivated and wild. The meadows of the White Carpathian Mountains are filled with multicolored wildflowers including many species of delicate orchids. Some farmers plant poppy fields. These flowers have large red or white petals with lots of small black seeds in the flower's center. The seeds are edible. When the flowers die, the dried black poppy seeds are shaken out and used in breads and baked goods. Chamomile is another popular and useful flower. Like the poppy, it grows well in hot sunny areas. The small flowers look like miniature daisies and grow quickly and easily. The dried flowers are brewed to make a soothing tea. Both chamomile and poppy "reseed" themselves. They drop seeds

A family picks poppies from a field.

constantly during the growing season. Because they are always dropping seeds, there is rarely, if ever, a need to replant these flowers. They grow back year after year in large numbers. In fact, they can take over areas quickly, so they have to be pruned, or pulled out of the ground. Pruning allows the remaining plants enough space to grow big and strong.

Chamomile and other flowers are used as medicinal herbs. Herbal medicine is popular in the Czech Republic. People may use a single herb, such as chamomile, or they might combine several to create a blend. Herbs are consumed in a capsule or steeped into a tea. People visit special pharmacies to purchase herbal blends that may heal anything from headaches to high blood pressure.

Where there are flowers and fruit orchards there are also bees. And where there are bees there is honey. Farmers commonly keep beehives in fruit orchards because the bees pollinate crops. The extra bonus is delicious honey. The flavor of honey depends upon the type of flower nectar the bees drink. There are more than 60,000 beekeepers in the Czech Republic tending nearly 600,000 beehives. The Bee Research Institute located in the small village of Dol assists beekeepers throughout the country. They supply queen bees (needed for every hive), visit hives that might be having problems, and help farmers maintain safe beekeeping practices.

A beekeeper inspects his hives.

National Zoo

The Prague Zoo (Zoologická Zahrada Praha) located in Prague, the capital city of the Czech Republic, has hundreds of species of animals. They include penguins, lions, sea lions, elephants, and some exotic wild goats with long horns such as the ibex. The flood of 2002 severely damaged the zoo. Hundreds of animals had to be temporarily moved. Workers and volunteers struggled to save as many animals as possible. About 100 animals died in what has been the worst tragedy in the zoo's history. Money and resources from around the world have helped rebuild the facility and return the animals to their zoo home.

Forests

During the communist years, many forests were cut down to make way for large cooperative government-owned farms. Today, about 34 percent of the country is still forested. There are softwood conifers such as pine, spruce, and fir trees. These trees are "evergreen," meaning they keep their needles and stay green all year long. There are also many hardwood deciduous trees like oak and maple, whose leaves change color and drop off in the fall season.

Both hardwood and softwood trees are used in the timber industry. Lumberjacks set up camp in the forests, cut down trees, and transport the logs on large trucks. Sawmills prepare the logs for manufacturing. Everything from furniture to paper to barrels for storing wine and beer is made from trees. Some trees also produce resin, a sticky sap that oozes from pine trees. Resin is used to make glue and varnish.

Forest Wildlife

Of course, forests not only provide raw materials for the timber industry, forests are home to animals and insects. Animal habitats depend on elevation, soil, and climate. The higher up

Protecting Plants, Animals, and Humans

Among the national parks in the Czech Republic is the Šumava National Park that is also a UNESCO Biosphere Reserve. UNESCO stands for the United Nations Educational, Scientific, and Cultural Organization. The Biosphere Reserves project seeks to preserve areas in the world that have important biodiversity (a variety of wildlife) and to promote sustainable development. The organization protects wildlife but also considers the needs of people. In this way, UNESCO seeks to create a better balance between man and nature.

Šumava National Park was once a royal forest and has remained in its natural state for hundreds of years. There are beech and fir trees that reach an amazing height of 200 feet (60 m) with diameters of up to 6.6 feet (2 m). Some of the trees in this park are believed to be thousands of years old. Rare flowers, birds, and animals also make their home in what is one of the oldest mountain areas in the Republic.

A lynx belongs to the cat family.

in the mountains you go, the more harsh the environment, the fewer the plants, and the more hardy the animals. Some creatures cross into several geographical zones while others live only within one zone.

In the lower mountain forests you'll find a wide variety of furry, four-legged creatures such as foxes, wolves, lynx, and bears—most of them live in the protected reserves and parks. That's a good thing because hunting is a popular sport. The bear has almost been hunted to extinction. But thanks to new government policies that protect threatened species, animals such as the nearly extinct bear are increasing in number every year.

Wolves hunt small animals in Czech forests.

The Czech Republic has many different kinds of birds including eagles, falcons, geese, vultures, owls, and storks. Trout and carp are in rivers and ponds. Beavers make their homes in the rivers of Moravia. There are plenty of reptiles, such as toads, frogs, salamanders, and snakes, that skitter around the rivers and forests, too. The only poisonous snake found in the Czech Republic is the viper. It likes sunny and wet places such as rocky riverbanks and ponds.

A salamander warms up on a rock.

Castle for the Birds

Bird watchers flock to the castle grounds in Lednice, Moravia, home to hundreds of birds including gray herons, Syrian and middle spotted woodpeckers, and collared flycatchers. Lednice leads the country in having the most bird reserves. Bird watchers from around the world come to see the feathered beauties and to listen to their lovely songs.

Butterflies are a common sight wherever there are wildflower meadows such as the hillsides of the Carpathian Mountains in Moravia.

The Czech Republic keeps a close count on its wildlife. Thirty-six globally threatened animals and fifty-two threatened plant species live in the country. Laws protecting rare plants and animals are firmly in place.

The Kladruby

The Czech Republic does not have an official national animal but it does have a cherished and very special horse called the Kladruby. The breed is a blend of Spanish and Italian horses that originated in the sixteenth century. This elegant, strong horse is typically black or white. It is used in sporting competitions and to pull carriages for special ceremonies. The horses have also captured the eye of filmmakers. The Kladruby appeared in the 2001 feature film, *A Knight's Tale*, starring Heath Ledger, Rufus Sewell, and Shannyn Sossamon. The horses were ridden in the jousting scenes.

FOUR

Roots of History

The history of the Czech people stretches back hundreds of years. For most of those years, Czech land was under foreign control. Germans, Austro-Hungarians, and the Soviets have all ruled this region. Prior to 1993, the Czech Republic was linked with Slovakia (now also an independent entity). Combined, the country was known as Czechoslovakia. Today, however, the Czech Republic is an independent republic. Historically, the Czech people have rarely enjoyed complete independence, making this current period of sovereignty especially sweet.

Opposite: **In 1989 people gathered in Prague to demonstrate for national freedom.**

Mythical Beginnings

The actual beginnings of the Bohemian Přemysl dynasty are unknown. So, an early Czech writer named Kosmas (1045–1125) made up a mythical tale that has been passed down through the generations. The legendary story involves a countess by the name of Libuš who ruled the Bohemians during the ninth century. She eventually married a common plowman named Přemysl. It is from their union that the first Czech royalty descended.

According to another legend, a mythical figure called Čech led the first Slav migration into northern Bohemia. The word "Czech" is derived from his name.

Legend aside, it is known that from the fourth to the sixth centuries, tribes were migrating and settling in various parts of

Čech and His Wandering Brothers

Czech people love their legends and one seeks to explain the origin of the word *Czech*. The story goes that three brothers, Čech, Lech, and Rus, wanted to find a new place to live. So they set out wandering with their tribes. Rus liked a place near the Dnieper River and settled there with his tribe, the Russians. Čech and Lech moved on to Bohemia. Reaching the top of a hill, Čech surveyed the beauty of the land and declared it the perfect place for his tribe. Brother Lech settled in the region that is present-day Poland.

Europe. Slavic tribes settled around Moravia and Bohemia in the sixth century. The most significant settlement was the Kingdom of Samo in Moravia. The people called themselves Moravians, after the name of the local river, Morava.

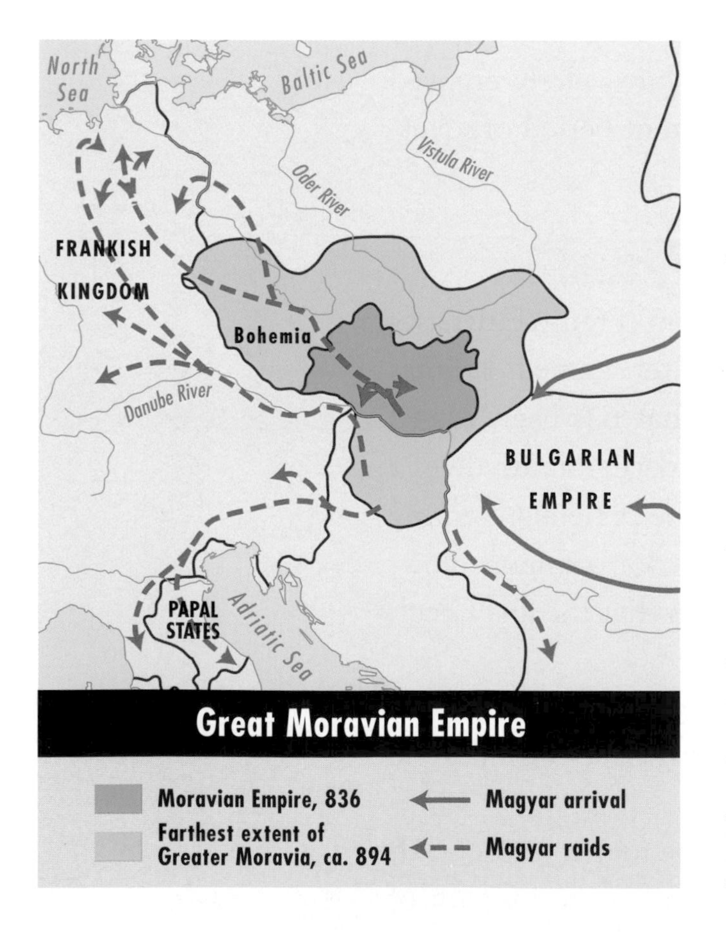

By the ninth century the Great Moravian Empire was established. The empire, under the rule of Mojmír I, held a great expanse of land including what is today known as Slovakia, Bohemia, and parts of Hungary, Poland, and Germany.

Around 894, the Magyars (later known as Hungarians) invaded Bohemia and Moravia from the southeast. The Germans feared the Magyars would extend their invasion to German land. The Germans joined forces with Bohemia and Moravia to fight against the Magyars. The Magyars, however, succeeded in

The Magyar invasions destroyed the Great Moravian Empire.

conquering Slovakia and a large slice of Moravia. This conquest ended the Great Moravian Empire. The slice of Moravia not captured by the Magyars linked with Bohemia and remains so to this very day.

Upon the collapse of the Great Moravian Empire, control of the region shifted from Moravia to Bohemia. Bohemia remained a German protectorate for a long time. The Bohemian Přemysl dynasty ruled Bohemia and Moravia in 950 and beyond, but they had to answer to Germany's King Otto I. This arrangement with Germany lasted until 1306. During this period, many Germans moved to Bohemia, making it their home.

Good Prince Wenceslas

Though known in the Christmas carol as Good *King* Wenceslas, he was actually not a king but a prince. Wenceslas I (907–929) was a member of the Přemysl dynasty who was known for his peaceful rulership style based on Christian values. Rather than fight with the Germans, Wenceslas I believed in negotiated settlements. His brother, Boleslav, disagreed with his methods and had him murdered. In the eleventh century, Wenceslas I was given the title of patron saint of Czech lands. He remains the Patron Saint of Bohemia.

King Charles IV and the Golden Age

The Bohemian Přemysl dynasty came to end when Wenceslas III was assassinated in 1306. There was no heir apparent, so rulership of the region passed to the Luxembourg dynasty. The first ruler, John of Luxembourg, wasn't very interested in governing Bohemia, but he did make some territorial gains. He eventually passed the throne to his son, Charles, better known as Charles IV. Charles was the king of Bohemia from 1346 to 1378. He further expanded land holdings and became the

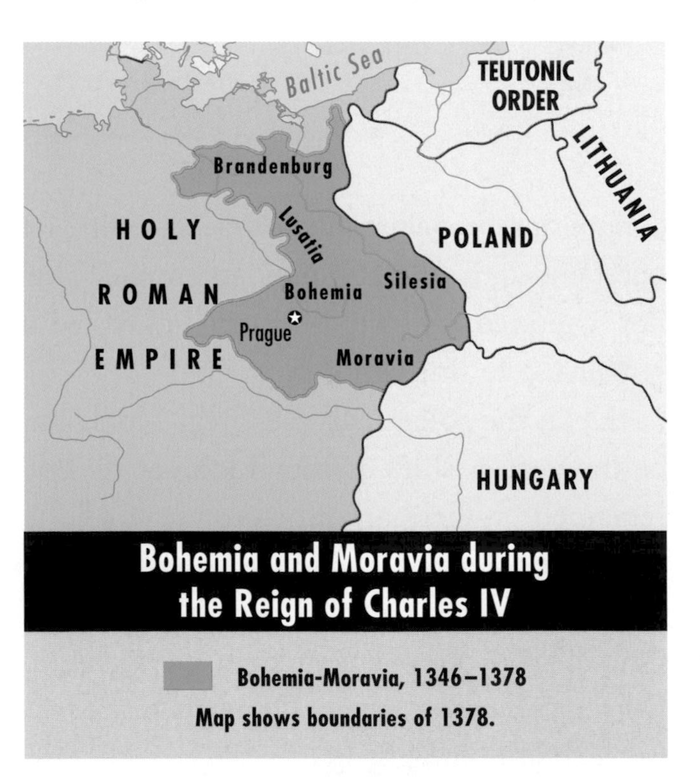

The famous Charles Bridge was built in the fourteenth century.

king of Germany in 1347. He ruled over many lands and was crowned as emperor of the Holy Roman Empire in 1355.

Under Charles IV, Bohemia blossomed into a cultural and political powerhouse. Prague became the second most important city in Europe, after Paris. He founded the famed health spa city, Karlovy Vary (Charles Spa), a town within Prague (Nové Mésto), restored the Hradčany castle and Saint Vitus Cathedral, and built the impressive Charles Bridge that linked the city's east and west banks. To safely store royal jewels and other wealth, he built a huge castle (Karlštejn) just outside of Prague. Education was also at the forefront of Charles IV's accomplishments. In 1348 he established the first university

Charles IV opens the first university in Central Europe.

in central Europe, Charles University, which attracted artists and intellectuals from all over Europe.

Charles IV was both French and Bohemian. He was raised in France but clearly dedicated his later life to Bohemia and all things Czech. He mandated that all government officials speak Czech and saw to it that church services would also be in the Czech language. Prior to that, German was commonly spoken in political arenas and Latin was the official language of the Roman Catholic Church.

Charles IV supported reformist religious leaders who believed the current church was corrupt and morally declining. The reformers called for a simplified version of early Christianity. Charles' support enabled the religious reformist movement to expand and gave rise to one the most influential religious and political figures in Czech history, Jan Hus, who led a rebellion against the Catholics.

The Habsburg Dynasty

The crown was available in the early 1500s when internal conflicts and the death of King Louis at the battle of Mohács left Bohemia without a ruler. The Catholic Habsburgs of Germany promised religious tolerance. But when they achieved rule in

A depiction of the Thirty Years' War "Battle of White Mountain"

1526, they quickly took back their promise. This angered the Protestant Czechs. For the next century, the Czechs and Habsburgs were constantly at odds. This led to the Thirty Years' War, which destroyed much of the economy and ended in the defeat of the Czechs at the Battle of White Mountain in 1620.

Afterwards, the Habsburgs assumed complete control of the region. They took away property, burned books, forced the Czechs to convert to Catholicism, and reinstated German as the official language. They ruled for 300 years. It was a period considered by the Czechs as the Age of Darkness because much, but not all, of Czech cultural life was in a deep sleep.

National Consciousness Reawakens

During the 1800s, Czech identity reawakened through the work of writers, politicians, and composers. Czech architecture flourished with the building of the National Theater and the National Museum in Prague. This awakening was due in part to the reign of Habsburg Empress Maria Theresa (1740–1780) and her successors. They eased the heavy hand of oppression and instituted educational reforms.

The process of building a modern Czech state took time and considerable effort. Three vital factors fostered Czech independence: revival of the Czech language, rather than German, as the official language, the formation of clear and unified political goals for independence, and control of the economy. All this would come to pass, but not without conflict and more periods of foreign occupation.

Empress Maria Theresa led the way to cultural and educational reforms.

The First Republic

The dawning of the twentieth century was a time of relative stability and peace in Bohemia and Moravia. The Habsburg Empire combined with the Austrians and Hungarians to become the Austro-Hungarian Empire. But by 1914, peace was over. Austria's Archduke Francis Ferdinand was assassinated, an event that snowballed into World War I. Many

Father of the Nation

František Palacký was among the most influential Czech intellectual of his time. He was a historian, poet, and politician who wrote *History of the Czech Nation*. The first volume of his work was published in 1836. He planted the seed for Czech and Slovak unification, something that would occur a century later. Palacký is fondly remembered as the father of the Czech nation.

countries entered the conflict. In the end, the war severely crippled the Austro-Hungarian Empire.

Once ruler of the land, the Austro-Hungarian Empire was now unable to exert much influence over its subjects. It was the perfect time for the country to declare independence. But even with a weakened Austro-Hungarian Empire, Czechoslovakia needed other powers to back her. When Czechoslovakia declared independence, the Allied powers of France, Great Britain, the United States, Italy, and Japan all stood behind her. On October 28, 1918, the Austro-Hungarian Empire unconditionally accepted the terms of Czechoslovak independence.

Allied Powers

The Allied powers are a group of countries that banded together in military alliance in order to fend off other countries. During World War I, the Allied powers consisted of twenty-eight nations and included Britain, France, Russia, Italy, and the United States; they opposed Germany and the Austro-Hungarian Empire.

In World War II some of the players changed sides. The Allied powers included Britain, the United States, and the Soviet Union, but this time they unified against Germany, Italy, and Japan.

The Republic's first president, Tomaš Masaryk, addresses his country.

Thousands of people gather to usher in independence in 1918.

Many people worked very hard to gain Czechoslovakia her independence. Chief among them was a university professor, Tomaš Garrigue Masaryk, who became the new Republic's first president. Prague was designated as the capital city.

Crowds flocked to the streets in celebration of their independence. However, the newly independent republic would not remain so for very long. While it lasted, however, Czechoslovakia prospered culturally and economically.

As a democratic society, there was more emphasis on sharing resources and knowledge. The Czechs and Slovaks learned from each other and from the countries around them. There was already some industry in the Czech lands at this time. But with independence, Czechoslovakia focused on creating new business opportunities and on exporting more of their products.

But Czechoslovak independence didn't just create new business opportunities, it was a time of change for society as a whole. People from all ethnic groups now had the legal right to a basic education. Free expression allowed the arts to flourish. Czechoslovak painters, writers, and musicians began to be recognized throughout Europe. Physical education became more important. Sports such as soccer and ice hockey began to gain in popularity. The talented Czechoslovak ice hockey team won a number of European championships during the country's early days.

World War II

In addition to Slovaks and Czechs who lived in Czechoslovakia, there were large groups of Germans. During this period Adolf Hitler and his party, the Nazis, were in political power in Germany. Sudetenland sat on the border of Czechoslovakia and Germany. It belonged to Czechoslovakia but most of the people who lived there were German and many wanted Sudetenland to be a part of Germany. Hitler insisted that Sudetenland historically belonged to Germany and demanded to have it back. Czechoslovakia appealed to the Allied powers for help. What happened shocked Czechoslovakia and forever changed her course of history.

In 1938, the Allied powers, namely Britain and France, signed an agreement with Hitler called the Munich

Agreement. It gave Sudetenland to Hitler. Czechoslovakia could hardly defend herself against the decision of these larger powers, so it had to give up Sudetenland. In protest to the decision, the Czechoslovak president, Edvard Beneš, went into exile in London. The Allied powers sold out his country and he needed help. He turned to the Soviet Union.

Why did the Allied powers give Sudetenland away? They thought they were putting a stop to Hitler's dreams of a greater Germany because in the Munich Agreement Hitler promised he would not invade Czechoslovakia. Unfortunately, he lied. In 1939, Hitler annexed all of Czechoslovakia. The Nazis completely took over the government. They removed Czechoslovaks and inserted German officials in their place. Czechoslovakia was under foreign rule once again.

German troops occupy the town square in Rumberg.

The Nazis occupied and terrorized Czechoslovakia. Colleges and universities were closed. It was illegal to assemble in groups. Nazis forced Jews into ghettos and concentration camps. During Hitler's invasion, an estimated 100,000 Jews, as well as those who opposed the Nazi party, were sent to concentration camps. By the end of Hitler's reign, 90 percent of Czech Jews had been murdered.

One particularly gruesome event paints a picture of what life was like under the Nazis. When Czechoslovak resistance fighters killed the German governor of Prague, Reinhard Heydrich, the Nazis retaliated by wiping out the entire village of Lidice. They killed all of the men, sent the women to concentration camps, and gave the children to German families.

Hitler, of course, didn't stop with Czechoslovakia, he invaded many other European countries. In 1945, Czechoslovakia was finally liberated from the Nazis with help from the United States and the Soviet Union. However, Czechoslovakia would soon find herself under foreign occupation again.

Warsaw Pact

In 1955, Czechoslovakia joined the Warsaw Pact, a "treaty of friendship, cooperation, and mutual assistance" among Communist member states. These states included the Soviet Union, Poland, Albania, Bulgaria, Hungary, East Germany, and Romania. Among other privileges, it allowed the Soviet Union to set up military bases in these countries.

Communist Rule (1948–1989)

Czechoslovakia was grateful to the Soviet Union for freeing her from the Nazis. Many Czechoslovaks thought Communism might benefit their country. When the Soviets entered, Czechoslovakia was a democracy. Unlike the United States, which has two primary political parties, Republicans and Democrats, the norm in Czechoslovakia was to have several competing political parties, including a Communist Party. At election time, many Communists were voted into office.

Name Game

Czechoslovakia had several different official names during the twentieth century. At first union, they were called the Czechoslovak Republic; in 1948 under Communism, the People's Republic of Czechoslovakia; in 1960, Czechoslovak Socialist Republic. In 1993 the Czechs and Slovaks went their seperate ways to form two independent countries, the Slovakia Republic and the Czech Republic.

In 1943, President Edvard Beneš signed a friendship treaty with the Soviet Union. By 1948, however, Communists and non-Communists in Czechoslovakia strongly disagreed with each other. The Communists had more power and were supported by the Soviet Union military.

Klement Gottwald, a Communist, was the prime minister. Gottwald believed that industries should be tightly controlled by the state. He led the way for the government to take over privately owned Czechoslovak industries. This angered many people, including the non-Communist government officials. Many politicians resigned in protest. They did that so new elections could take place and the Communists could be voted out of office. The Communists, in turn, staged violent rallies. They took control of the election process and placed only Communist names on voting ballots. The Communist Party, called the National Front, won the elections.

The Communists wrote new laws that would make their party even more powerful. Beneš refused to sign the new legislation. He was forced to resign and Gottwald became the new president. Gottwald turned Czechoslovakia into a one-party Communist state. It was, in essence, a Communist dictatorship.

Local politicians followed the command of Soviet Union leader Joseph Stalin. The Soviet Union was the headquarters of the Communist Party that dictated how the country would be governed. The iron fist of Communism came down hard on Czechoslovakia. It became a game of life and death to speak against the Communists or Russia. If you were merely suspected of being a Communist Party traitor, you could be put in jail, work camps, or executed.

Communists organized society according to what was called a Socialist system. Under this system, the government "nationalizes" the country. The idea was that the government (and therefore, in theory, the people) would equally share wealth and resources. In Czechoslovakia, the government took over banking, factories, farms, stores, and transportation systems. There was no such thing as freedom of the press. The only newspapers were state owned, and printed only positive stories about the government. Just about everything was state owned. No one could own property. All land was taken away from private farmers and turned into state collective farms. Many people left the country rather than be subjected to such oppressive rule.

Prague Spring

Socialism isn't just one absolute organizing model for society, there are different forms. Under Communism, this social structure tended to be very controlling, but even within Communism there are degrees of strictness. By the 1960s, Czechoslovaks wanted more freedoms. Freedom of speech, a free market economy (the Soviets regulated and set prices for

Alexander Dubček calls for social reform.

wages, goods, and services), influence over how business was run, and other freedoms were desired.

In 1968, Alexander Dubček, was elected as the leader of the Communist Party. He advocated "socialism with a human face." He reformed government policies. People enjoyed more freedom than they ever had during the twenty years of Communist rule. At last, the press was free to express honest political opinions, and they did. The press often criticized what was wrong with Communism and Russia. Czechoslovaks could travel freely to other countries. They were free to assemble in groups. The Soviets were not pleased.

The Soviets worried that they were losing control of Czechoslovakia. If Czechoslovakia was able to have a more liberal government, other Communist countries might want the same. The Soviets met with Dubček and insisted that he revoke his liberal policies. Czechoslovaks protested in the streets, but demonstrations were illegal according to the Soviets. On August 21, 1968, Warsaw Pact armies, under the command of the Soviets, marched into Prague with tanks leading the way.

The Soviets invade Czechoslovakia in 1968.

Dubček and other government officials were arrested. Dubček was forced to sign the Moscow Protocol, which stated that he agreed to the Soviet military presence in Czechoslovakia. The Protocol also took away his liberal policies. The military stayed in Czechoslovakia to crush any further rebellion.

The Czechoslovaks had tasted freedom but it had all too quickly been pulled away. One young student, Jan Palach, was so depressed by what happened to his country, that, in protest, he set himself on fire in front of the National Museum. Thousands left the country. The people would, however, demand their freedom again.

In 1977, Czechoslovakian writers and intellectuals created Charter 77. It was a document that criticized the oppressive Communist government policies. The exceptional boldness behind Charter 77 was that people actually signed their names to it. Remember that Communists imprisoned people who criticized the government. Signing Charter 77 was extremely brave. Some members, including playwright Václav Havel, were sent to prison for signing it. But the ball of freedom was rolling again and this time is would not be stopped.

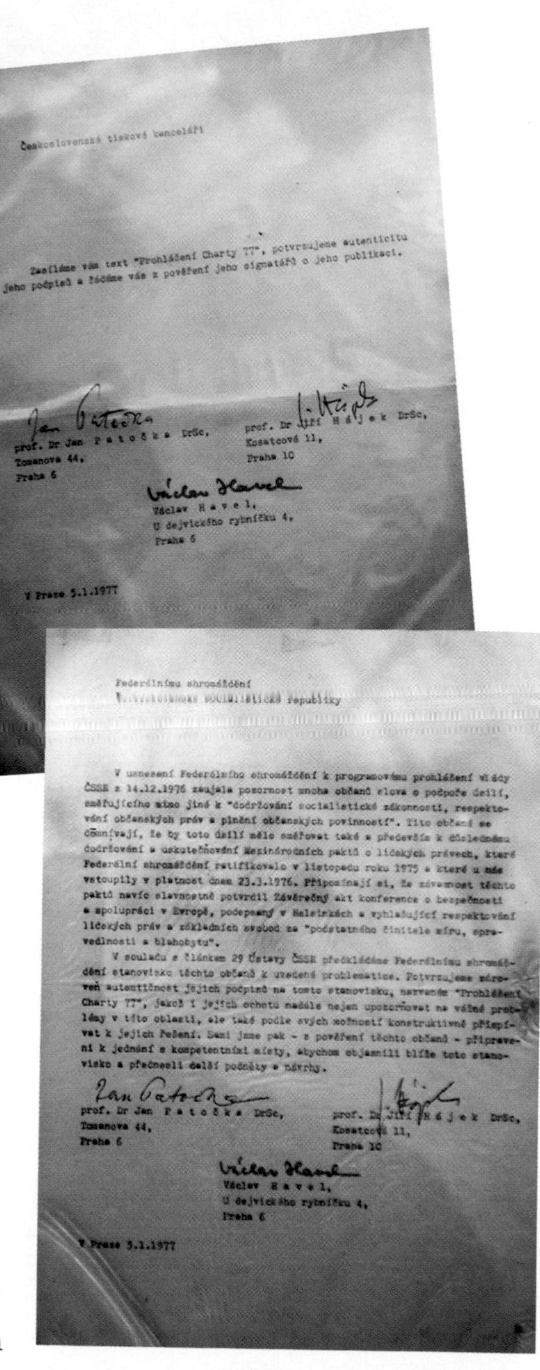

Československá tisková kancelář

Zasíláme vám text "Prohlášení Charty 77", potvrzujeme autenticitu jeho podpisů a žádáme vás z pověření jeho signatářů o jeho publikaci.

prof. Dr Jan P a t o č k a DrSc,
Tomanova 44,
Praha 6

prof. Dr Jiří H á j e k DrSc,
Kosatcová 11,
Praha 10

Václav H a v e l,
U dejvického rybníčku 4,
Praha 6

V Praze 5.1.1977

Federálnímu shromáždění
[illegible] socialistické republiky

V usnesení Federálního shromáždění k programovému prohlášení vlády ČSSR z 14.12.1976 zaujala pozornost mnoha občanů slova o podpoře úsilí, směřujícího mimo jiné k "dodržování socialistické zákonnosti, respektování občanských práv a plnění občanských povinností". Tito občané se domnívají, že by toto úsilí mělo směřovat také a především k důslednému dodržování a uskutečňování Mezinárodních paktů o lidských právech, které Federální shromáždění ratifikovalo v listopadu roku 1975 a které u nás vstoupily v platnost dnem 23.3.1976. Připomínají si, že závaznost těchto paktů navíc slavnostně potvrdil Závěrečný akt konference o bezpečnosti a spolupráci v Evropě, podepsaný v Helsinkách a vyhlašující respektování lidských práv a základních svobod za "podstatného činitele míru, spravedlnosti a blahobytu".

V souladu s článkem 29 Ústavy ČSSR předkládáme Federálnímu shromáždění stanovisko těchto občanů k uvedené problematice. Potvrzujeme zároveň autentičnost jejich podpisů na tomto stanovisku, nazvaném "Prohlášení Charty 77", jakož i jejich ochotu nadále nejen upozorňovat na vážné problémy v této oblasti, ale také podle svých možností konstruktivně přispívat k jejich řešení. Sami jsme pak - z pověření těchto občanů - připraveni k jednání s kompetentními místy, abychom objasnili blíže toto stanovisko a přednesli další podněty a návrhy.

prof. Dr Jan P a t o č k a DrSc,
Tomanova 44,
Praha 6

prof. Dr Jiří H á j e k DrSc,
Kosatcová 11,
Praha 10

Václav H a v e l,
U dejvického rybníčku 4,
Praha 6

V Praze 5.1.1977

Charter 77 is a letter that openly criticized Communism.

People protest against the government in Prague 1989.

The Velvet Revolution

During the late 1980s, the Soviet Union was also changing. A more progressive leader, Mikhail Gorbachev, was in charge. He instituted many reforms that affected Communist member states, including Czechoslovakia. Hope for independence was rising. When Czechoslovak independence became a reality, it happened quickly and without violence. That's why it was called The Velvet Revolution. It was smooth and elegant.

The pivotal event occurred in November 1989. Crowds gathered in Prague to pay respect to students who had been killed years before by the Nazis. College students, the vocal changemakers in Czechoslovakia, organized the gathering in Prague's Wenceslas Square. Chants for freedom filled the air. For several days, more and more people took to the streets. Václav Havel, released from prison after four years, made a moving speech. It rallied the crowd to strike, meaning people would stop working. They did and the Communist government began to crumble.

In the meantime, Communism was on the decline elsewhere in Europe as well. When Germany's east and west sides were rejoined, citizens tore down the Berlin Wall, a barrier between Communist East Germany and independent West Germany. When the Czechoslovaks rose up against Communism, the Soviets did not invade Prague as they had years before. It was a peaceful parting of ways. In December 1989, Václav Havel was elected president. Communist rule in Czechoslovakia was finally over. Change and challenge awaited the new leaders.

The Velvet Divorce

The vast majority of people were certainly happy to see the end of Communism. But there was tension between the Czech and Slovak side of this dual republic. Much of it stemmed from economic policies. The Havel government moved quickly toward privatization—he returned businesses, farms, and property to private citizens. At the same time, he reduced military spending. The main industry in Slovakia was building arms and this reduction severely hurt the Slovak economy. Furthermore, independence ruined the relationship Slovakia had with Russia, who bought a lot of Slovak steel and agricultural products. Slovakia's economy was shrinking while the Czech economy was improving.

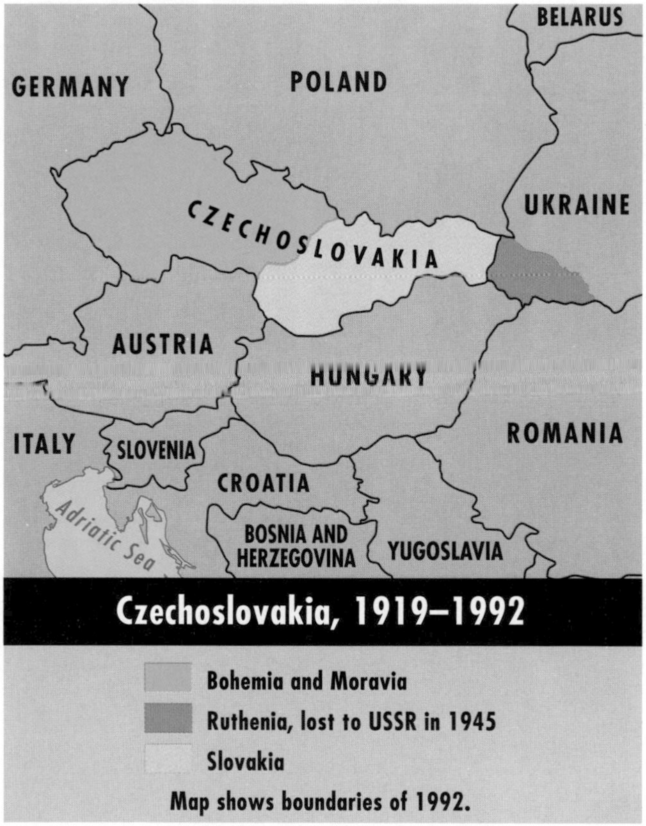

Slovakia had often felt second-best to the Czech side of the Republic. The economic differences between the two republics made things worse. By the early 1990s, there was a growing movement for an independent Slovakia. In January 1993, they got their wish. Owing to the nonviolent nature of the breakup, the split was labeled the Velvet Divorce.

Czechoslovakia, 1919–1992

Bohemia and Moravia
Ruthenia, lost to USSR in 1945
Slovakia
Map shows boundaries of 1992.

Building an Independent Republic

The first step to any meaningful changes . . . must be a fundamental change in the social climate of the country, which has to regain a spirit of freedom, trust, tolerance, and plurality.
—Václav Havel, Wenceslas Square, 1989

THE ROLE ORDINARY CITIZENS PLAYED IN THE CREATION OF an independent Czech Republic cannot be overstated. All in the quest for human rights and freedom, many lost their jobs, some suffered years in prison, and some lost their lives. Without massive public protest, the Communist government would likely still be in charge today.

Opposite: **The Czech Republic's national flag represents pride of country and independence for all Czechs.**

The people of Czechoslovakia proved that governments could be dismantled and changed. But it takes effort, time, and persistence. The payoff is independence. However, change has its hardships. This became evident when the Czech Republic and Slovakia parted ways after seventy years together. It took a long time for the split to be finalized because the two republics shared many common resources such as the Czechoslovak military. There were also disputes about property and business ownerships. It was a complicated, but civil divorce.

On December 16, 1992, a new constitution laid the groundwork for the parliamentary democracy of the new Czech Republic. The new constitution emphasized human dignity and freedom as vital rights for all citizens. The Czech

Republic (*Ceska Republika*) became a fully independent republic in 1993. The government structure is a parliamentary democracy. The new Czech leaders have been hard at work to institute all kinds of reforms including social, political, and economic. The challenges have been many.

A Government Defined

A parliamentary government consists of a bicameral (two-part) legislature with a chamber of deputies (lower house) and a senate (upper house). In the Czech Republic there are 81 senate seats and 200 chamber seats. The members of both are elected by popular vote. Czech citizens over the age of eighteen years are entitled to vote. Senators serve six-year terms and deputies serve four-year terms.

A parliamentary democracy differs somewhat from the presidential democracy that is the U.S. government model. The main difference is in the office of the president itself. In the Czech Republic, and other parliamentary-styled governments, it is not the president who holds the most power, it is the prime minister. The prime minister, however, is appointed by the president so the two would have similar political philosophies.

Compared to the United States, how the president is elected into office differs as well. In the United States the president is elected via the electoral college system. In contrast, in the Czech Republic, the president is elected by members of parliament. A Czech president serves a five-year term and cannot serve more than two consecutive terms.

From Playwright to Prisoner to President

Václav Havel was born into wealth and privilege in Prague on October 5, 1936. At that time, Czechoslovakia was an independent republic and people owned private businesses. His father was a well-respected businessman who owned property, restaurants, and other establishments. When the Communists took over in 1948, the Havel family, like most wealthy families, were stripped of their businesses and respected positions. Unless they joined the Communist Party, they were forced to work jobs far below their skill and ability. Businessmen and other professionals found themselves washing windows, picking up garbage, and performing other tasks.

Because of his high income, Havel was rejected from many schools. He wanted to attend art school but was denied entry. Instead he went to a technical school for carpentry. Despite the educational restrictions placed on him, however, Havel found his true love in life, theater, and the written word.

In 1959, Havel became a stagehand for the ABS theater company in Prague. He adored the theater, wrote many plays, and gained significant attention for his work. In 1968, during the Prague Spring, a time when freedom of speech was allowed, he and others spoke out against the Communist regime. But before long, the Communists cracked down. They tried to silence him by banning his plays and removing copies of his work from libraries and bookstores. Instead of keeping quiet, Havel dug in his heels and became more vocal about the injustices of the government. He was imprisoned several times. His plays gained international attention and won important awards. His views were now heard beyond Czechoslovakia. The government had to be careful in their dealings with him. Havel had a following and the international community was watching. The Communists told Havel he could freely leave the country (but not come back). It was their attempt to get rid of this nonconformist who was becoming too popular. Havel stayed.

Havel believed it was his life's work to protest against human injustice in Czechoslovakia. As founder of Charter 77, he discovered that many Czechoslovaks believed as he did. In 1989, nearly a half a million people protested in Prague. It was the final blow to the Communist government. In the past, they had squashed protests by sending in police with clubs and tear gas to disperse the crowd. This time there were just too many people. The Communist government resigned. Havel was appointed as president of Czechoslovakia. When the two republics split, he was elected president of the Czech Republic in 1993, and reelected to a second term in 1998.

Václav Havel has been recognized as an international hero for remaining true to his convictions and for never settling for less than what he believed. He followed his heart and led his country to independence.

Vladamír Špidla became prime minister in 2002.

The Czech Republic president is the official head of state but his powers are rather limited. He is the commander-in-chief of the military, appoints the prime minister, has veto power (but parliament can override it), represents the country in foreign affairs, and can grant amnesty (pardon prisoners and others charged with crimes). Václav Havel served as president from 1990 to 2003. He was the president of Czechoslovakia and when it dissolved he was reelected as the president of the Czech Republic.

The prime minister is more responsible for the day-to-day running of government. He is the leader of the majority political party in parliament. Vladamír Špidla became the Czech prime minister in 2002.

The cabinet of ministers help run the country.

The prime minister recommends a cabinet of ministers who must be approved by the president. The cabinet includes such members as the ministers of justice, education, culture, transportation, finance, and health. Each minister is an expert in his or her field. The ministers help the prime minister develop new laws and amend existing ones. All legislation must pass through both chambers of parliament to become official.

The Czech Republic has a multiparty political system. After Communism ended, there were more than 100 political parties vying for government seats. Today, there are far fewer parties but still more than the United States, which has two powerful parties,

NATIONAL GOVERNMENT OF THE CZECH REPUBLIC

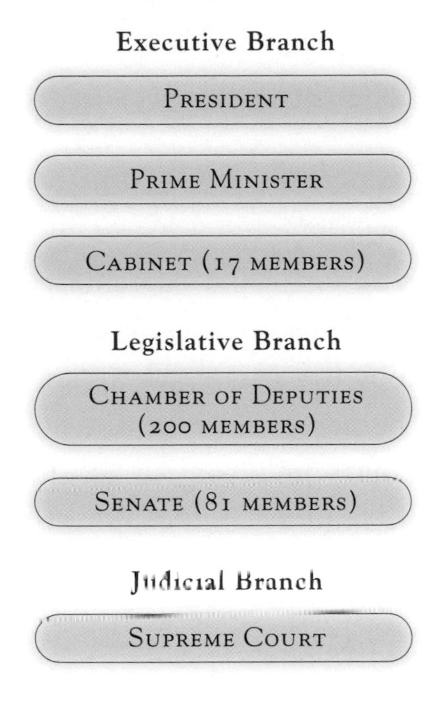

Democratic and Republican. There are more parties in the Czech Republic than in the United States, but they are far weaker, and exert little influence over political races for office. Compare that to the Czech Republic, where there are many parties active in the parliament. The largest are the Czech Social Democratic Party and the Civic Social Democratic Party; these are followed by the Communist Party of Bohemia and Moravia, the Christian-Democratic Party, and the Civic Democratic Alliance.

Representatives of parliament (deputies and senators) are elected by the people using a secret ballot. They represent people from various regions. The Czech Republic has fourteen administrative centers. Those centers are further divided into smaller districts. District representatives handle local topics such as schools, roads, and utilities.

Judicial System

The department of justice has a hierarchical system. At the top are the constitutional and supreme courts. The Czech president nominates judges of these courts, but appointments must be approved by the senate. There are also regional and district courts. When problems arise, the first stop is generally a district court. Courts are organized according to need, such as civil, criminal, military, and administrative courts. For example, if a crime was committed, the parties would attend a

Of Flags and Symbols

The flag of the Czech Republic has two equal horizontal bands of red and white, a blue triangle is wedged between the two bands on the left side of the flag. In addition to the flag, the Czech state has a coat-of-arms. Coat-of-arms are old symbols that were used during the Middle Ages. They identified families, business ownerships, and kingdoms.

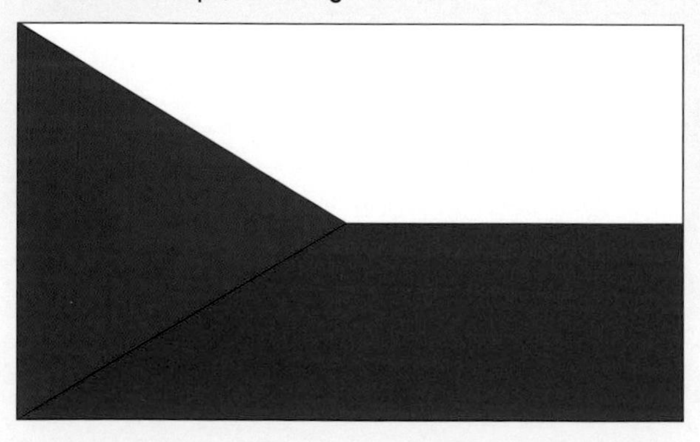

The Czech coat-of-arms is a symbol from the thirteenth century. The coat-of-arm is a shield divided into four parts. The upper left and lower right have the same image: the Bohemian white two-tailed lion with a gold crown. The lion represents strength and independence. The upper right corner has a red-checkered female eagle with a gold crown that is a symbol from Moravia. Appearing lower left is a black female eagle, also with a gold crown. The black eagle represents the small district of Silesia. Today, the Czech Republic sometimes uses just the Czech lion as a symbol for the Republic.

criminal court; for a business dispute the court of choice would be a commercial court.

Department of Defense

The Czech Republic has an army, air defense forces, internal security, territorial defense, and railroad units. Males over the age of eighteen must serve twelve months in the military. As of 1989, they could select nonmilitary service for twenty-seven months instead. The military has nearly 55,000 armed forces personnel, not including those who serve in civil defense units. The yearly defense budget is in excess of one billion U.S. dollars.

Keeping the country safe is a top concern and the responsibility of the National Security Council. The Council members meet several times a year to discuss the country's security issues. Article 1 of the Statute of the National Security council clearly states their mission:

> *Formation of a reliable national security system, to ensure co-ordination of and control over the measures aimed at safeguarding the security of the Czech Republic and international obligations.*

The Czech Republic became a NATO (North Atlantic Treaty Organization) member state in 1999. By doing so, it is part of an organization of countries that vows to protect any member whose sovereignty is threatened by outside forces.

Czech soldiers serve their country.

Prague: Did You Know This?

This magnificent city traces its roots back to the ninth century. The centuries-old palaces, cathedrals, and castles, along with modern cafés and shops, attract millions of tourists every year. Today, Prague is one of the most visited cities in Europe.

The city is 191 square miles (496 sq km) with a population of 1.2 million. Most of the people who live there are Czech but there are other minorities such as Slovaks, Germans, Romanies (Gypsies), and Jews. Prague is high on culture and many artists live, work, and spend time in the cafés. Since the fall of Communism, a growing number of Americans and British have also made Prague their home. In summer, many locals leave the city, preferring to spend time in their country cottages. The city is visited by 3 million tourists. Temperatures are quite comfortable in the summer, averaging around 68°F (20°C); in winter, the temperatures drop below 20°F (–6°C).

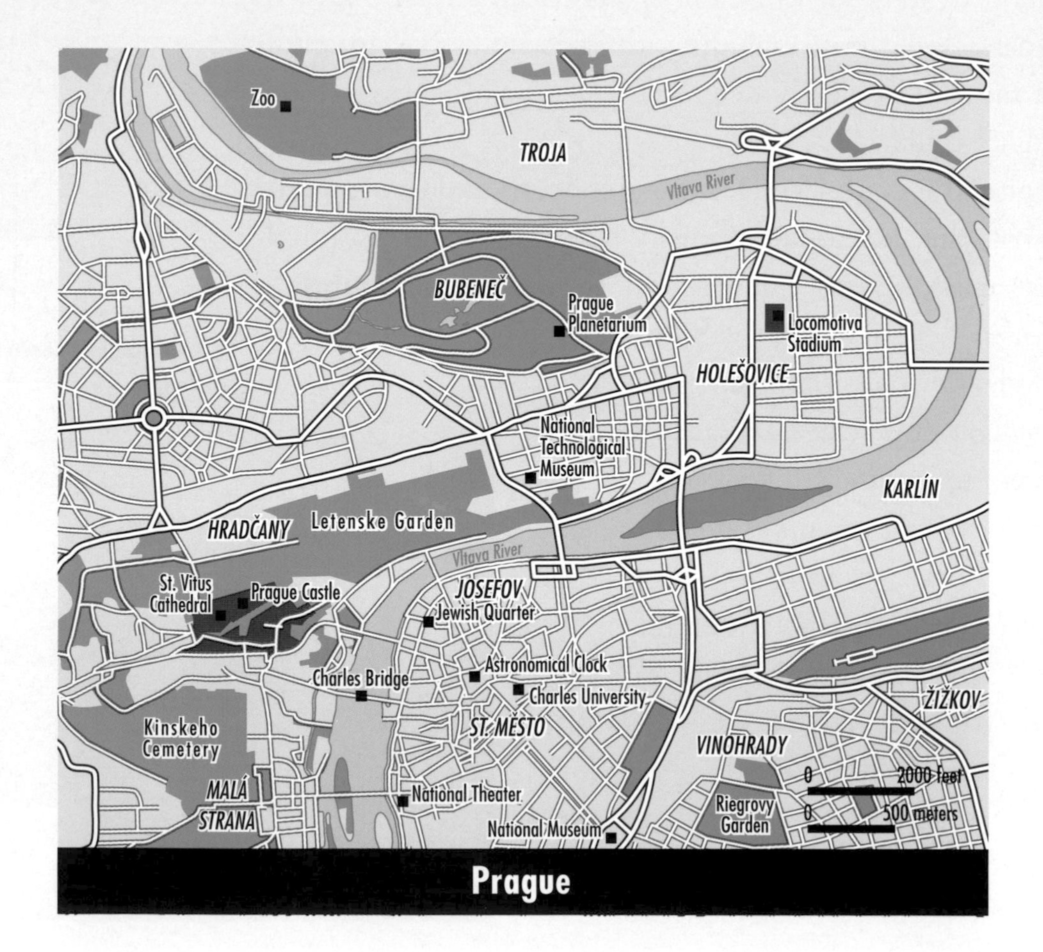

Prague

Modern transportation systems crisscross the city and include buses, railways, and taxis. Steamboats cruising down the Vltava River are popular with tourists. There are many glorious architectural sites to see in this city. Chief among them are the astrological clock (below) that includes twelve marching apostles

and a moving figure of death, and the Charles Bridge (above), a fantastic work of art built of stone and graced with thirteen statues of saints. The bridge links the old town to the new and is open to pedestrians only. Saint Vitus Cathedral is the centerpiece of the Hradčany castle (also called Prague castle) complex. Prague castle has long been the seat of government and is the residence of the Czech president today. Numerous buildings and pretty garden paths make up the castle complex.

Legends about this city abound. Among the most famous tales is that of the Golem, a man-made monster that haunts Prague's Jewish Quarter. Other ghouls and ghosts are said to roam the city, including one who sold his body to the university for scientific experimentation. This tall ghost haunts Charles University and begs for money so he could buy back his soul.

From Communism to Capitalism

THE CZECH ECONOMY HAS TRANSITIONED FROM COMMUNISM to capitalism. These are two completely different economic systems. The transition from one system to another takes time, patience, and careful planning. Think of the Communist economic system as threads woven into the fabric of Czech life. The threads must be carefully pulled out so that whole fabric doesn't fall apart.

Opposite: **Glass designers cut crystal in this Mozar factory.**

The Communist Economic Structure

During the years 1948 to 1989 the Czech Republic was part of Czechoslovakia and both were under Communist rule. Under a Communist system, the government controls businesses. The government was like the chief executive officer of all companies. It decided every aspect of how companies run. From wages to products produced, the government dictated all. This included how much products could be sold for, to whom products/raw materials could be sold, how much workers would be paid, which products/raw materials could be imported, and from whom those products/raw materials could be purchased. For the most part, Czechoslovakia traded only with other Communist states. This meant it could not sell products to wealthier neighbors such as Germany. This limited its profit potential. But in a Communist system that didn't matter much. Jobs and wages were virtually guaranteed for life. Workers didn't have to care about profits or efficiency, because everyone got paid no matter what.

These kinds of conditions didn't encourage workers to increase production or improve product quality. Even if workers had good ideas, they had little authority to make changes because the government held all the power. Despite all of this, Czechoslovakia was the most prosperous of all Communist states.

Pollution has become a real problem in the Republic.

Economic development during the Communist years centered around heavy industry. The Communists built a lot of factories, especially in the northern region. The factories extracted and processed natural deposits from the surrounding mountains. The mountains contain iron, coal, lead, and copper. Unfortunately, heavy metal factories produce lots of pollution. This is why much of the northern territory of the Czech Republic is heavily polluted. Today, environmental laws help limit pollution. Many of the old factories have been shut down because their processes and equipment are outdated.

Independence, Economic Reform, and Privatization

With independence in 1993 came economic reform. The Czechs have shifted from a government-controlled economy to a market-driven free enterprise system, also known as capitalism. This means that individual companies decide how to run their businesses. Supply and demand determines products, pricing, and wages. It also means that companies have to run much more efficiently than they did in the past. Business leaders and workers have to learn how to function under this new system.

Among the first tasks was to "privatize" businesses, factories, and farms owned by the government. Farmlands were returned to original owners or sold. Some factories and businesses were sold to foreign investors. Many foreign companies have invested in the Czech Republic. These businesses are attracted to the highly skilled Czech workforce that works for wages far below more developed countries. Nearly 40 percent of international investment has been in automotive production.

The Republic's central European location also makes it a highly desirable place to do business. During the early days of privatization, international businesses flocked to the Czech Republic. Some converted existing factories; others started new companies.

In addition to attracting foreign investment, the Czech government gave the Czech people an opportunity to invest in companies. For a small fee, Czechs received special vouchers which could be traded for stocks in a variety of companies. In a short time, many Czechs owned stock for the first time in their lives.

A business woman runs her own flower shop.

The opportunity for growth under the capitalist system is strong. Of course, this business system meant that wage and job security, once common during the Communist era, were now gone. Factories and companies that were unproductive closed down. But Czechs welcomed the challenge. Growth has been good, and unemployment remains low.

Once again, Czechs could start their own companies. Small and mid-sized businesses sprung up countrywide. Restaurants, cafés, and small private shops were popular new businesses. The capital city of Prague especially prospered in the early days of reform.

The transformation is far from over. Economic reform is a slow process loaded with risk and reward. Compared to other post-Communist countries, the Czech Republic is doing quite well and serves as a good role model for others.

Joining the European Union

The European Union (EU) was established in 1993. As of 2002, there are fifteen member states in the EU. It is a structure that seeks to unite European countries under a common umbrella. The idea is that in unity there is strength.

Among the first tasks of the EU was creating a common currency. The monetary unit known as the euro is the result. The euro replaced individual country currencies and has simplified international trade and accounting.

The Czech Republic is applying for membership in the EU. The benefits of membership are many. As a member, the Czech Republic could buy and sell products and services with other member states more easily. Membership would also improve cultural and social relations with other EU countries. The Czechs hope to join the EU in 2004.

Agriculture

In general, the agricultural sector is not very productive. Czech agriculture makes up about 5 percent of GDP (gross domestic product). About 3.7 percent of the population is employed in the agricultural sector.

The soil is certainly fertile, but agriculture as a large-scale business is unorganized. The methods for distributing farm goods is especially lacking. This disorganization is due in large part to the Communist economic system of the past. People got paid more to work in factories than to farm. Therefore, many people abandoned farming. Food was imported from other Communist countries so the Czech Republic didn't worry much about producing its own food. Now that the Republic is independent, it imports a lot of its

Gross Domestic Product by Sector

Industry	41%
Services (2000 est.)	35%
Agriculture	5%

The government helps farmers with economic incentives.

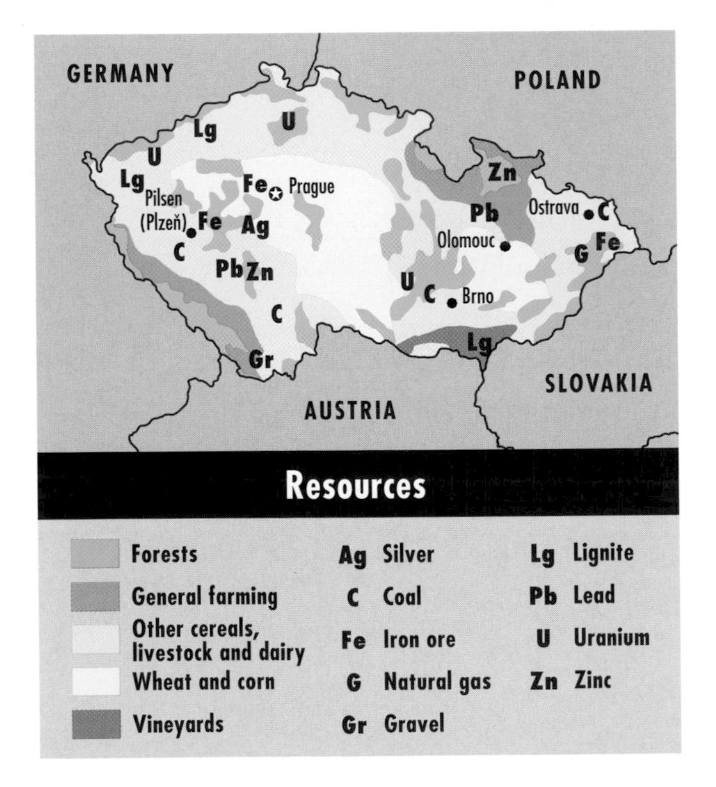

food and for prices above those it used to pay under Communism. Food has become more expensive for everyone. To help reduce the dependence on food imports, the government has put incentives in place to encourage farming.

The main crops are sugar beets, potatoes, wheat, and hops, a grain used to make beer. The Czech Republic is one of the world's largest producers of pilsner beer, and it is considered among the finest beers in the world. It is exported to many countries, including the United States.

International Praise for Czech Wine

The tradition of Czech winemaking goes back to the third century. The hills and valleys of Moravia are ideal for growing grapes. Ninety-seven percent of the Republic's wine is produced in Moravia; the remaining 3 percent of the wine is produced in Bohemia. Some of today's vintners (winemakers) have won international awards for their fine wines.

The Czech Republic imports more than 50 percent of the wine it consumes. At present, there are 32,000 acres (13,000 ha) dedicated to vineyards. The government wants to expand the winemaking sector and has offered farmers attractive incentives to cultivate vineyards. Their goal is to double the current wine production.

Manufacturing

Manufacturing is a leading industry in the Czech Republic. Forty-one percent of the country's labor force is employed in this sector. Historically, the Czech Republic has been a major manufacturer of weapons. As far back as the Habsburg Empire, the Czech Republic was producing military equipment. In the 1980s, as Czechoslovakia, it was one of the world's largest arms exporters. Today, however, the Czech Republic does not export weapons.

Czech factories process raw materials and make finished products. Factories process iron, steel, and other metals. Some factories construct large machines that make items such as shoes and wood products. These automated machines are

What the Czech Republic Grows, Makes, and Mines	
Agriculture	
Wheat	4,084,000 metric tons
Barley	1,629,000 metric tons
Sugar beets	2,809,000 tons
Manufacturing	
Bicycles	229,377
Trucks	23,641
Woven fabrics	226,088,000 metric tons
Mining	
Brown coal and lignite	50,307,000 metric tons
Hard coal	14,855,000 metric tons
Kaolin	1,242,000 metric tons

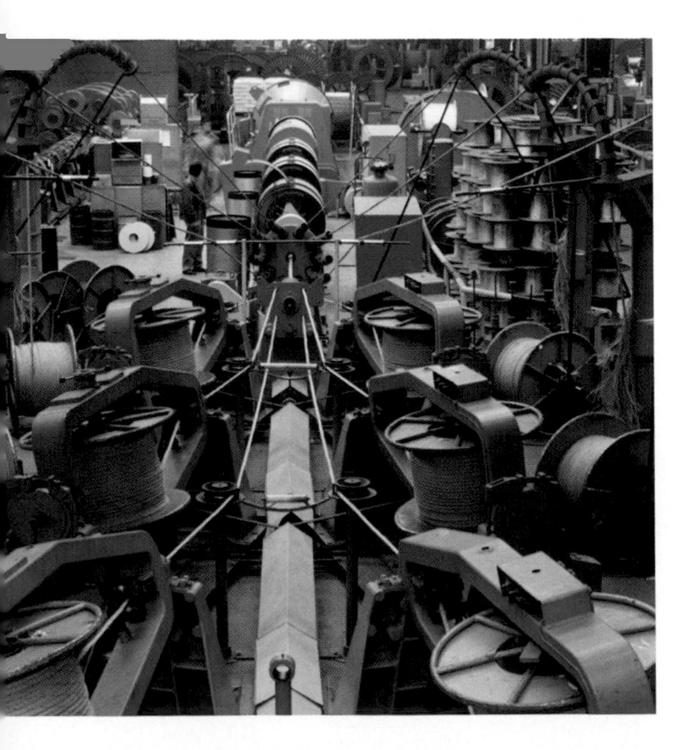

A factory manufactures cable.

exported to other countries around the world. Czechs also make many finished products including transportation vehicles, tools, chemicals, electronics, glass, jewelry, beer, foods, and pharmaceuticals. Czech crystal is considered among the finest in the world. Crystal glasses, vases, and bowls are sold in small roadside stands as well as large department stores.

The service sector includes many different kinds of businesses. Among them are banking, health care, and tourism. Catering to tourists is among the fastest developing service sector of the Czech economy. About

Summer tourists crowd the Charles Bridge in Prague.

100 million tourists visit the Republic every year. Prague is by far the most popular city. Many cafés, restaurants, hotels, and specialty tour services have opened to specifically meet the needs of tourists. The health spas west of Prague are the second most visited area in the Republic.

Weights and Measures

The Czech Republic uses the metric system. Most countries use it for common weights and measures. Units include kilogram for weight, kilometer for distance, meter for length, liter for liquid volume, and Celsius for temperature.

Trading Partners

The Czech Republic buys and sells goods with many countries. Here's a breakdown of what the Republic exports/imports and from whom. Compared to the Communist era, it is a far different trading structure.

Export partners	
Germany	40.4%
Slovakia	7.7%
Austria	6.0%
Poland	5.4%
UK	4.3%
Export commodities	
machinery and transport equipment	44%
intermediate manufactures	25%
chemicals	7%
raw materials and fuel	7%
Import partners	
Germany	26.7%
Russia	6.4%
Slovakia	6.0%
Italy	5.2%
Austria (2000 est.)	4.9%
Import commodities	
machinery and transport equipment	40%
intermediate manufactures	21%
raw materials and fuels	13%
chemicals	11%

Energy

The Czech Republic imports most of its oil and gas from Russia. It generates most of its electricity from coal, nuclear, and some from hydro (water) plants. The nuclear plant in

Temelin is located on the border with Austria and has been controversial. The construction of the plant was started during the Communist era. Austrians and some environmental groups claim it is unsafe. They want the plant shut down. The Czech government insists that the plant is safe and that it has been upgraded to reflect current standards. The debate continues.

Some people believe the Temelin nuclear plant is unsafe.

Czech Currency

The basic units of currency are the heller and the koruna, meaning crown. There are 100 hellers in one koruna. Coins are minted in values of 10, 20, and 50 hellers and 1, 2, 5, 10, and 20 korunas. Paper banknotes are printed in denominations of 20, 50, 100, 200, 500, 1,000, 2,000, and 5,000 koruna notes. One U.S. dollar is worth approximately 30 korunas.

Czech banknotes have many elements that make the paper money difficult to forge. There are watermarks that are visible when held against light, special metallic strips, and orange threads woven through the paper.

All the Czech coins carry imprints of the numeric value and the distinctive Czech lion. One side of each coin has been designed by a famous Czech artist. For example, the 5 koruna coin was created by sculptor Jirríí Harcuba. His design includes the famous Charles Bridge and the river Vltava.

CHAPTER SEVEN

Origins of Language and People

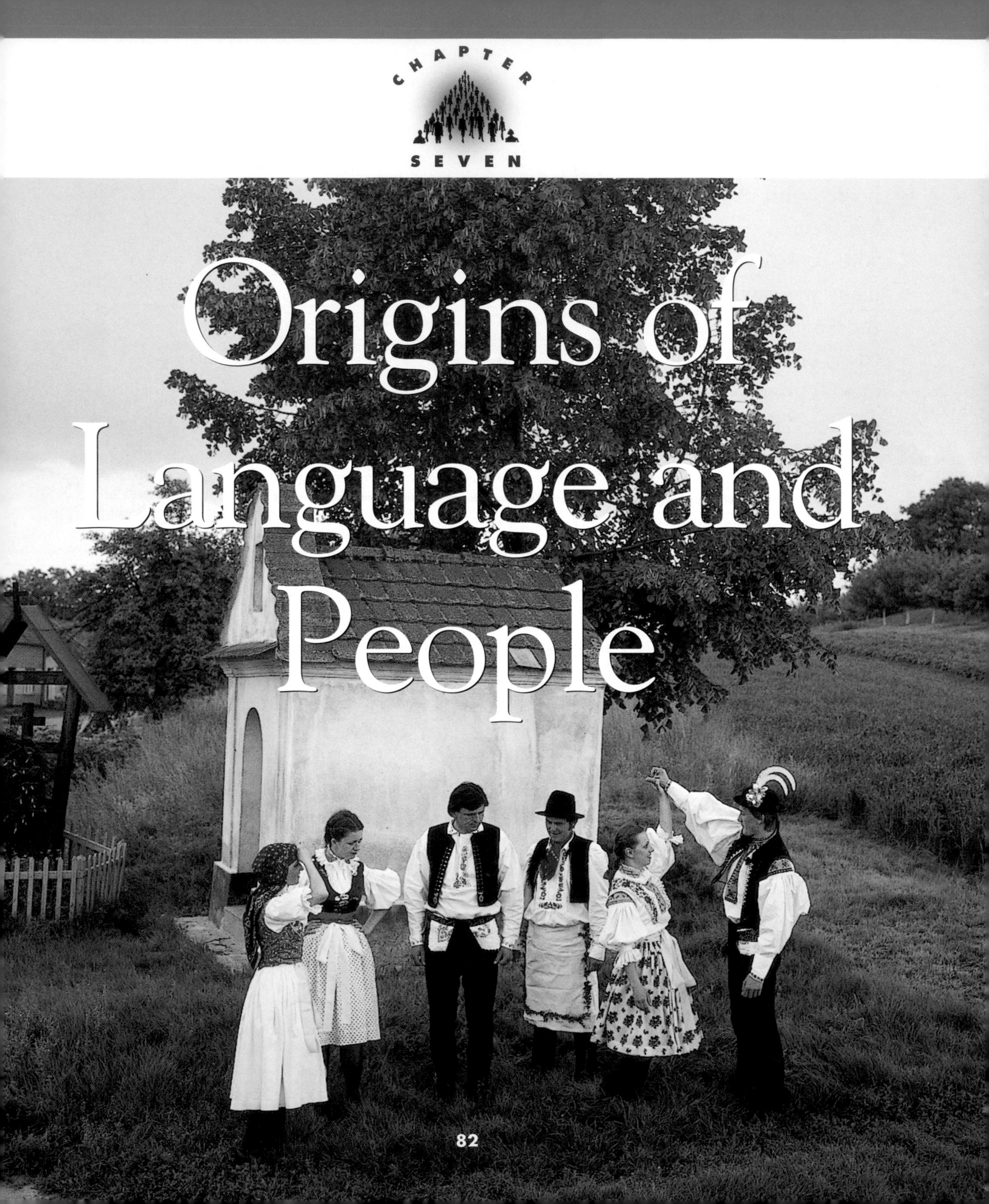

In 1980, the Czechoslovak government was building a new expressway in the town of Beroun, about 19 miles (30 km) west of Prague. While digging up the earth, workers found ancient tools shaped from animal bones. It turns out these weren't just any old bone tools. They dated back to the earliest Paleolithic period, making them about 1.8 million years old. The tools were made by *Homo erectus*, a relative of modern humans. But this was not the only evidence of early human life in what is now known as the Czech Republic. Remains from Neanderthals have been found in Moravian caves, and descendants of modern humans dating back to 40,000 B.C.E. have been found in Konéprusy caves.

Opposite: **Czechs in national dress get ready to dance.**

Tribal Migrations

In the sixth century B.C.E. a tribe with Celtic origins lived in the region. They were called the Boii tribe and they were quite industrious. They built hillside forts, used the pottery wheel to make functional yet decorative ceramics, and worked with bronze and iron. They organized their communities around forts, establishing the first urban centers. Their language was the foundation of all Latin-based languages, such as English and German. In fact, the word "Bohemia" is derived from Boii. This tribe dominated the region for hundreds of years.

The next influential group entered the scene around the first century C.E. They were Teutonic (German) tribes. During this period, the Roman Empire was also expanding. These two groups fought each other in Southern Moravia. But they didn't battle alone for long. Other migrating peoples joined in the fight for land and dominance.

From the fourth to the sixth century, Europe was awash with migrating people. Whole tribes, including Slavic groups, were on the move. A major instigator of all this movement was the Huns, an Asian tribe that pressured other tribes to migrate. The Huns were constantly attacking the Roman Empire that by this time had expanded into much of Europe. The most notorious Asian leader was Attila the Hun. After his death in 453, the Huns gradually lost power.

Slavic groups, who eventually became known as Czechs, settled in the region around the fifth century. Several hundred years later, in the ninth century, they had quite a powerful nation. It was located in the western part of the Czech Republic, Moravia.

Politics, Language, and Religion

It is impossible to separate the development of the Czech language from politics and religion, as they have been intertwined for centuries. In fact, the first written Slavic language was introduced to the Czechs by religious missionaries. The request for the missionaries came from a political leader.

During the middle of the ninth century, the Great Moravian Empire was under its second ruler, Count Rotislav (846–870). Fearing a takeover by the Germans, Rotislav positioned himself with the Eastern Roman Empire. At Rotislav's request, the Eastern Roman Empire sent missionaries to

Saints Cyril and Methodius created the Slavic alphabet.

spread Christianity to the people. The missionaries were Greek brothers named Cyril and Methodius. These brothers had invented the first Slavic alphabet, Cyrillic, and a church language called Old Slavonic. They introduced the written Slavic language to the Czechs.

Common Czech Terms and Phrases

Prosim	Please
Dekuji	Thank you
Ano	Yes
Ne	No
Ja	I
Matka	Mother
Otec	Father
Anglicky	English
Dobry den	Good Day
Na shledanou	Goodbye
Nerozumím.	I do not understand.
Jak se máte?	How are you?

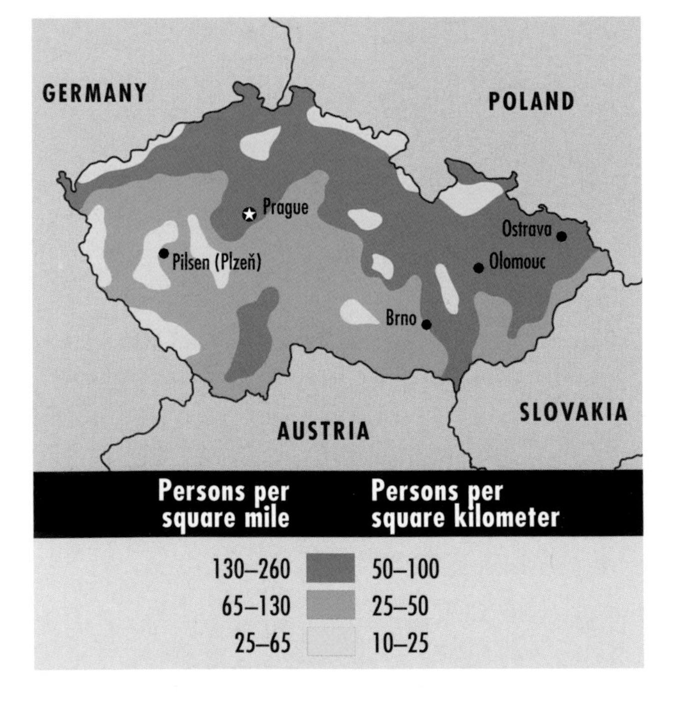

Around the eleventh century, religion would again influence language. This time, Latin became the official church and literary language, replacing Old Slavonic. A few hundred years later, in the fourteenth century, Jan Hus, an important political and religious leader, further refined the Czech language. Hus organized the various Czech dialects by forming a common spelling. The language developed further under the reign of King Charles IV, who also built the first university.

Through the centuries, the Czechs have had many foreign rulers. The Germans and Russians in particular have greatly influenced the language and life in the Czech Republic. That Russian and German shaped some aspects of the Czech language cannot be denied. But in addition to influencing Czech, both German and Russian have been official languages spoken in the Czech Republic. At the end of the eighteenth century, German became the official state language under the German-speaking Habsburg Empire. When Germany occupied Czechoslovakia in the mid-twentieth century, German again became the official language of government and business. When the Communist Russians marched in, they made Russian a required language in all schools.

The People of the Czech Republic

The Czech language is closely tied to Czech identity. When the Republic sought independence as a distinct nation, it pointed to its language as a unique identifying factor. Today, Czech is the official state language as decreed by the government. German and English are also widely spoken, especially by those working in the tourism industry. There are many English language schools in the Republic. In spoken Czech, it is not unusual to hear some English and German words sprinkled into the conversation.

A common language is a major contributing factor to unity and identity.

Pubs like this one in Prague are popular gathering places.

Today, pubs and cafés are centers for socializing, especially in the cities. Beer and music are often a part of these gatherings. For example, when musicians in pubs play folk songs it is not unusual for Czechs to join in singing.

There is a strong love of nature among the Czech people. Many city dwellers have country cottages to which they escape most weekends, especially during the summer. Czechs are also quite proud of their nation's artistic and intellectual accomplishments. Many Czech artists and scholars are known worldwide. As a whole, Czechs tend to be well educated and knowledgeable about world events. Czech schools are excellent and many people speak at least two languages. The literacy rate is nearly 100 percent.

Ethnic Breakdowns	
Czech	4.4%
Slovak	3%
Polish	0.6%
German	0.5%
Gypsy (Roma)	0.3%
Hungarian	0.2%
Other	1%

How Czech Differs From Other Slavic Languages

The Czech language is a Slavic language. Slavic languages traditionally used the Cyrillic alphabet that was introduced by monks in 863. Because of the influence of the Roman Catholic Church, the Czechs adopted the Latin alphabet during the Middle Ages. The Czech language also has a different speech pattern than some other Slavic languages. The "r" sound is unique and has no English equivalent. It is often described as soft and gurgling. Emphasis is on the first syllable and the rhythm of the words and sentences have a harder, more staccato beat, an influence from the German language.

Ethnic Groups

The majority of people who live in the Czech Republic are Czech and 70 percent of them live in larger towns and cities. There are, however, other ethnic groups who make their home in the Republic. Many Germans settled in border towns between the Czech Republic and Germany. The Republic also has a Slovak, Polish, Gypsy (called Roma), and a small Vietnamese and Jewish population. Because Judaism is a religion whose members come from many nations, they are not statistically counted as a separate ethnic group.

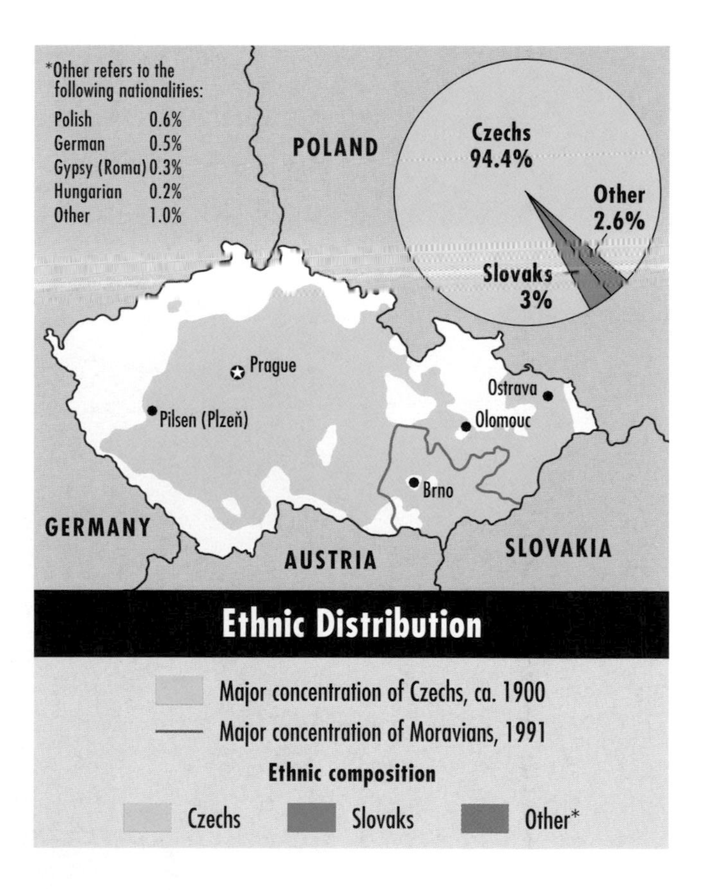

Jews have lived in the Czech Republic as far back as the tenth century. Under the Roman Empire, Jews were segregated into a gated community in Prague. A wall surrounded this community

The crowded Old Jewish Cemetery, Prague

to contain the Jewish population. It was a town within a town, with its own rules and customs. Though much of this ghetto has been torn down, the overcrowded Jewish cemetery still exists. At one time, Jews could only bury their deceased in this one cemetery—it is Europe's oldest and best-preserved Jewish burial ground.

Today, Jews and other groups live where they please. The number of Jews in the Republic is far less than what it was before World War II. During Hitler's rampage, an estimated 100,000 Jews from the Czech Republic were murdered.

Czech Republic's first Jewish primary school

Gypsies celebrate their heritage at the Czech Republic's World Festival of Gypsies.

Descendants of Germans have lived in this region since the first century. They arrived before the Slavs. Germans have influenced much of Czech life from language to politics to business and education. Before 1945, there were nearly 3 million German natives living in the region. Many, however, were expelled due to concerns about their ties to Hitler. Today, a controversy still exists over land that once belonged to these deported families. The Czech Republic borders Poland on the northeast. It is here where most of the Polish minority live. The town of Tesin has the highest percentage of ethnic Poles.

The Gypsies, or Romany, are believed to have migrated to mainland Europe from India before the fourteenth century. Their lifestyle has been traditionally a nomadic one, moving from place to place in groups. Today, they live in settled communities. Romany are especially known for their exceptional music and dance skills. The census numbers don't reflect the reality of how many Romany live in the Czech Republic. Many people prefer not to list Romany as their ethnic origin, fearing discrimination.

Population of Major Cities

Prague (Praha)	1.2 million
Brno	388,596
Ostrava	325,827
Pilsen (Plzeň)	171,908

CHAPTER EIGHT

Beliefs, Traditions, and Superstitions

GLORIOUS CHURCHES AND CATHEDRALS STAND AS PROOF that religion has played an important role in Czech society. Today, however, churches are more likely to be filled with tourists than with worshipers. Nearly 40 percent of the Czech population claims they are atheists. Atheists don't believe in God or are unsure that God exists. How did so many people become atheists in a land where there are so many churches? For the answer to that question, we need only step back a few decades.

Opposite: **A stunning stained glass window at Saint Vitus Cathedral**

Communists Oppose Religion

During the Communist years (1948–1989), the official religion of the land wasn't a religion but a philosophy called atheism. The government wanted to have as much control over people as possible, which included control over what people believed. The church, of course, had its moral teachings and spelled out how people should behave. This placed religion and the Communist government in conflict with one another. Because the government wanted people to be loyal to it first and foremost, it chose to minimize the importance of religion.

To achieve this, the government assumed authority over churches. They removed established church leaders and installed new ones. Clergymen were allowed to conduct only certain ceremonies, such as marriages. Sermons were essentially banned or restricted to particular subjects. By

Religious Practices in the Czech Republic

Atheist	39.8%
Roman Catholic	39.2%
Protestant	4.6%
Orthodox	3%
Undecided	13.4%

A Pope Visits

Pope John Paul II visited the region in 1997 and was welcomed by a large group of people. Pope John Paul II is Polish and therefore of Slavic descent. He is the first Slavic pope in history. The Czechs felt a special pride having a Slav in such a powerful religious position.

The Pope had two main purposes for his visit. One was to celebrate the Bohemian Saint Adalbert, who was the first bishop of Prague. The second was to usher in the first of a three-year period of preparation for what the Pope called the Great Jubilee of the Year 2000.

In his departure speech, the Pope had a special message for the young people of the Czech Republic: "I entrust to Saint Adalbert, the great son and heavenly Patron of this land, the aspirations and the future of the entire Czech People, and I express the hope that the younger generation will be worthy of the historical heritage of which they are the bearers."

suppressing religion, Communists could better control and build a society in the way they believed best.

It was not illegal to go to church, but it was discouraged. An entire generation of Czech people grew up in a society where religion was thought to be unimportant. That is why so many people today are atheists. Of course, there is another sizeable part of the population that does affiliate itself with a religion, mostly as Roman Catholics. Historically, certain governments and ruling empires helped promote Catholicism as the Christian religion of choice.

Christianity Through the Centuries

In the ninth century, Christianity was introduced to the region by Cyril and Methodius, two missionary monks from Greece. The Czech region was a part of the Holy Roman Empire. When the Empire split into two parts (called the Great Schism of 1054) the Czechs remained aligned with Rome. As such, they were Roman Catholic Christians (as opposed to Eastern Orthodox Christians). They remained Catholic until the religious reformer, Jan Hus, entered the scene.

Church and state were closely aligned during the Middle Ages. In 1380, a deadly plague claimed lives across Europe. The religious reformers in the Czech Republic saw this horrible event as God's punishment for the declining morality in the Catholic Church. Some people believed the plague was the end of the world. Many in the religious community felt a need for change.

Jan Hus emerged as the leader of a Christian reformist movement. He and his followers believed that the church had diverted from original teachings of Christianity and had become corrupt. They sought to right the wrongs of church and state. Many people joined Hus in his beliefs. He became

Roman Empire Times Two

The Roman Empire was initially based in Rome. Eventually it had so much territory that it needed two administrative centers to control it all. The main administrative center was based in the Empire's capital, Rome, Italy; the other was in Constantinople (today's Istanbul, Turkey). By the fifth century, Constantinople became more powerful and took control from Rome to become the capital of the Empire. These two centers would eventually split from one another in a move called the Great Schism of 1054.

quite influential. Too influential, according to the Catholic pope. He was told to stop preaching. Hus continued to preach and was excommunicated (expelled) from the church. Hus met with the church council to explain his point of view. But the council demanded that he recant his position, meaning he'd have to say his views were wrong. He refused. He was burned at the stake for heresy in 1415.

Hus became even more popular after his death. His followers, called the Hussites, rampaged through the country destroying Catholic symbols. In 1419, a radical Hussite group stormed the New Town Hall in Prague and tossed Catholic leaders out the window. A revolution was under way. Known

Birth of a Leader

Jan Hus was born in 1373 in Husinec, a small village in Bohemia. He studied liberal arts and theology at Prague University. He joined the church and became quite a devoted priest. Eventually, Hus became the head priest of the University and gave his sermons at the Bethlehem Chapel in Prague. He gained a popular following among the Czech people and became the priest to which Queen Sophie made her confessions. His devotion to the Roman Catholic Church was quite strong until it became apparent to him that the church had become corrupt. In 1402, he began to preach against the corrupt ways and insisted that the word of God be spread in the native Czech tongue. Hus' position caused a huge rift between the Germans, who remained aligned with the Roman Catholic Church and the Czech people, who viewed Hus as an important leader for Czech identity in the German-dominated era.

Hussite soldiers battle against Catholics.

From Farm Tools to Firearms

The Hussite army consisted mostly of serfs (farmers). They fought with home-made weapons fashioned from farming tools like axes and reinforced carts. The mobile and light armaments worked well. Among their inventions was a small portable cannon, called a píst'aly. "Pistol" is derived from this word.

as the Hussite Revolution, the Hussites and Catholics battled each other for years. The Hussites were defeated in 1434. For two hundred years after that revolution, Bohemia remained anti-Catholic. The people became Protestants.

The term "Protestant" refers to Western Christians who are not Roman Catholics. The word is derived from the verb "to protest." That's what reformers such as Jan Hus did; they protested against a corrupt Catholic Church.

During the seventeenth century, the German Habsburg dynasty came to rule the Czechs. The Hapsburgs were Roman Catholics. They banned any other form of religion, forcing Catholicism on the people. It was not until the early twentieth century that the Czechs were free to worship as they chose. When the Communists took over in 1948, however, religious freedom was once again repressed.

Religions Today

The dominant religion in the Czech Republic is Christianity. Most Christians follow the teachings of the Roman Catholic Church. But there are other varieties of Christianity practiced, including Orthodoxy, Protestantism, and denominations such as the Evangelical Church of Czech Brethren and the Czechoslovak Hussite Church. There are also non-Christian based religions in Czech society such as Judaism, Islam, and Hinduism. Though some Czechs may claim to be a member of a religion, most do not attend regular church services.

Before the 1939 Nazi invasion of Czechoslovakia, there were some 360,000 Jews living in the country. Most were murdered. Today, there is a small community of about 10,000 Jews. Many of them live in the Josefov district in Prague. Jews have been living in the Czech Republic since the tenth century. Their house of worship is called a synagogue. One of

Europe's oldest synagogues built in the late thirteenth century is located in Josefov. It is open to visitors and continues to have regular religious services.

The Josefov synagogue is a fine example of Gothic architecture and remains a spiritual center for area Jews.

A Gothic Cathedral in Prague

Saint Vitus Cathedral is the largest in the Republic and is located within the Prague castle complex. It was under construction for nearly 600 years. Work began in 1344 under Emperor Charles IV, who wanted an honorable burial place for Czech patron saints. Many spiritual leaders as well as persons of royalty have been laid to rest in a mausoleum below the chapel. Wars and changes in rulership stopped construction at various periods in time. It was finally completed in 1929. Czechs take great pride in this architectural masterpiece. The cathedral has influenced Gothic architecture throughout central Europe. Thousands of tourists visit the cathedral every year.

Superstitions and Traditions

Holidays are a time of fun and feasting in the Czech Republic. Easter has a number of traditions, some which have nothing to do with religion. During Communism people rarely celebrated Easter in the traditional sense, rather there were customs associated with spring such as fertility rites. Today, women and girls paint Easter eggs on Easter Sunday. The boys, however, are busy preparing their whips for the next day. Easter Monday is "whipping day." On this day, boys whip girls with twigs from birch trees. Being whipped with a birch twig

Finely painted eggs are ready for Easter in the Prague Old Town Market.

Decorations are everywhere during Christmas.

is supposed to guarantee fertility. It is an age-old custom done in good fun with soft sapling twigs.

Christmas Eve, December 24, is the most festive of the Christmas holidays. It is the day people decorate their Christmas trees. Gifts are exchanged on this day, after the traditional dinner of fried carp and potato salad. Children believe that the Baby Jesus delivers the packages. During dinner, the father sneaks away to set gifts under the tree. After opening gifts, families attend midnight church services.

Christmas Eve is also a popular time for fortune telling. There are two common ways to foretell the future: with an apple and with lead. An apple is cut in half. If the core is shaped like a cross, it means bad luck; a star means good luck. People have also poured hot lead into a container of water. The lead figure that solidifies in the water is interpreted to tell the future.

Religious Holidays	
Easter	March or April
Cyril and Methodius Day	July 5
Jan Hus Day	July 6
Christmas Holidays	December 24 and 25

Pilgrimages to religious sites have been popular in the Czech Republic for many years. There are hundreds of sites around the Republic at which believers pray and tourists visit. The Virgin Mary is especially celebrated. She is said to have appeared in many places in the country bringing miracles, love, and faith. Her image appears in paintings and sculptures in most churches, chapels, and cathedrals. There are numerous holy days dedicated solely to her. There are also many legends such as the one at the Nativity of Our Lady Church. During reconstruction of this church, the Virgin's image was plastered over and painted. But in a short time, her original image is said to have magically reappeared through the thick layers of paint and plaster.

Worshippers gather to honor the Virgin Mary.

CHAPTER NINE

Artistic Souls

THE CZECH REPUBLIC WAS AND IS AN IMPORTANT CENTER for the arts in Europe. In fact, Czech culture can best be seen through its arts. The Republic is famous for its exceptional architecture, literature, theater, film, painting, and music. There is an old saying from the eighteenth century that defines just how deeply music is seeped into the Czech soul—"scratch a Czech and you'll find a musician." That means that just below the surface, Czech people have a special love and talent for music.

Opposite: **Folk musicians in Prague, Old Town Square, delight passerbys with traditional tunes.**

Musical Nation

As far back as the sixteenth century, Czechs received musical training as part of their daily education. At least one hour a day was devoted to musical instruction. Teachers, called kantors (Latin for "to sing"), could sing, compose music, and play a variety of musical instruments. In addition to lessons, teachers and students joined church, school, or community choirs. Every town had choirs, and singing was a popular activity for all. Even today, you'll find people in pubs singing folk songs along with the house bands.

Music in the Czech Republic flourished during the Baroque period (1600–1750). "Baroque" refers to a style of art that was bolder, more emotional, and more elaborate than the art that came before it. The Baroque art movement influenced music, painting, and architecture. Massive pipe organs were installed in ornately designed churches. The Church of Saint Maurice in Olomouc has a working Baroque organ that is still played during services and special occasions.

An organ fills the Saint James Church with a glorious sound.

National Theater

The Czech National Theater opened its doors for the first time in 1881. The first performance was an opera, *Libuse*, which is the story of the mythical princess of Prague who founded the city. The opera was composed by Bedřich Smetana. The original theater burned down but was quickly rebuilt and reopened in 1883. Operas, ballets, and plays continue to be performed here today.

Bedřich Smetana,
Czech composer

During the 1900s there were so many talented musicians that a historian called Bohemia the conservatory of Europe. Czech musicians were well respected for their talent and creative musical style. Several Czech composers gained international fame. Bedřich Smetana (1824–1884) was the among the first important classical composers to achieve world class status. He is best known for incorporating Czech folk music and fables into his classical compositions. He inspired many Czechs with his patriotic work entitled, *Má Vlast* (*My Country*), a series of symphonic poems celebrating the Vltava River and the Bohemian countryside. Smetana lost his hearing in 1874, went insane, and died ten years later.

Composer Leoš Janáčk

Composer Antonín Dvořák (1841–1904) was a violin player in the National Theater orchestra under the direction of Smetana. As a young man, he played the violin at his father's inn. He used the money he earned to attend music school in Prague. Dvořák's works were also infused with Czech folk life. He achieved international recognition for his compositions called *Moravian Duets and Slavonic Dances*.

Composer Leoš Janáčk (1854–1928) spent much of his early years transcribing folk songs. He also created a musical language for animal noises and the imagined sounds of nonliving things. He called this musical language Melodic Curves. He is most remember today for his opera *The Cunning Little Vixen*, and his choral work, the *Glagolithic Mass*.

Instrument Makers

The Czech Republic is known for fine-quality stringed instruments such as mandolins, guitars, and violins. In the early days, all instruments were handcrafted. The skill was passed down from generation to generation. Today, most instruments are factory made though there are still some specialty shops where instruments are made by hand. The first violin making school was established in 1908 in the small village of Luby. The tradition continues today. You can buy handmade violins from the highly skilled makers in Luby. It takes time, talent, and fine wood to make violins. Some are very expensive and sell for more than two thousand dollars each.

These days Czech musicians play everything from alternative to classical, techno, trance, jazz, and even Christian rock. Pop music of the Czech Republic is similar to the kind of music heard and seen on MTV. Some Czech bands use English names such as Jolly Joker and the Plastic Beatles of the Universe. A pop rock band by the name of Krystof has a singer that is the spitting image of the American actor Brad Pitt; another popular group uses a Christian-like name, the Ecstasy of Saint Theresa, but their trance music is nothing like faith-based Christian rock.

Literature

Literature is as important to the Czech soul as music. Czech authors have written in a variety of languages including Latin, German, and French. Why did they write in other languages? The main reason is foreign occupiers, such as the Germans and Russians, who passed laws requiring everyone to write and speak their languages. The earliest writings were religious texts and historical chronicles written in Latin. The Czech language got a boost from religious reformer, Jan Hus, who wrote Czech grammar books. Scholars in the nineteenth century developed the first extensive Czech language dictionary, inspiring many writers to create in Czech.

The Czech Republic is especially known for its creative writing such as poetry, short stories, plays, and novels. Jan Neruda (1834–1891) is considered among the greatest writers of the nineteenth century. He worked as a journalist but also wrote poetry and short stories. He, like many writers, wrote about what he knew. His *Tales of the Little Quarters* is a collection of stories featuring life in his hometown of Prague. Franz Kafka (1883–1924), on the other hand, is best known for his strange and surreal stories. For example, his story entitled *Metamorphosis* features a young man who wakes up one morning and finds that he has become a cockroach. Kafka was born in Prague but wrote his stories in German.

Prague cafés were and still are popular gathering places for writers and poets. Jaroslav Siefert (1901–1986) was a Czech poet who won the Nobel Prize for literature in 1984. Siefert frequently went to Prague's Union Café, a gathering place for artists in the early 1900s. Siefert and other Czech poets of the time were similar to some rap artists and poets today who use their words to speak out against social injustices.

Author Franz Kafka was famous for his eerie stories.

Another important writer was Karel Čapek (1890–1938). He wrote many different kinds of works throughout his career including travel essays, children's stories, novels, and essays. He was a close friend of President Masaryk and conducted many interviews with the president, recording his thoughts and the details of his life. Among Čapek's most internationally influential works was a play written in 1921 called *R.U.R* (*Russom's Universal Robots*). The play features a machine-like man. It is from this theatrical work that we get our word "robot."

Milan Kundera

Born in 1929 in Brno, Milan Kundera was educated in Prague. He wrote poetry, plays, fiction, and film scripts and has received many literary awards. His first novel, *The Joke*, was published in 1967. Communist censors banned it. It won the Czechoslovak Writers Union Award and was translated into twenty different languages. Kundera's 1984 novel, *The Unbearable Lightness of Being*, became a bestseller and was turned into an English language film in 1988. Kundera moved to France in 1975 to escape Communist censors. He became a French citizen and now writes mostly in the French language.

Working in the longer medium of the novel are well-known modern Czech novelists Milan Kundera, Ivan Klíma, and Josef Skvorecky. Of the three, only Klima stayed in the Czech Republic. Kundera and Skvorecky left to escape Communist censorship. Today, artists and writers are free to express themselves as they please. Many people around the world appreciate Czech writers. Czech books are translated into other languages more frequently than writers from other countries.

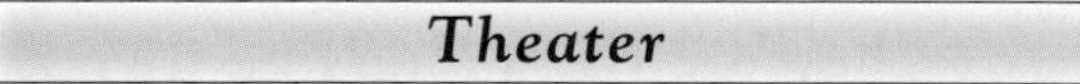

Theater

The Czech Republic has had no short supply of interesting theater. Marionette (puppets on strings) theater goes back to the sixteenth century. Troupes toured the countryside to present live drama to villages that did not have theater. The troupes used puppets to tell stories of Czech history as well as to perform dramas and comedies.

Puppet theater continues to be popular today. Works performed include fantasy, unusual, and classical stories. Czech fairy tales commonly feature a devil. But rather than being an evildoer, the Czech devil is more a foolish fellow. A more unusual form of puppet performance is luminescent theater. It involves coating costumes with a special glowing paint. The coated characters perform under an ultraviolet black light producing quite an eerie effect. The National Marionette Theater uses life-sized marionettes that perform serious classical works such as Mozart's opera, *Don Giovanni.*

Czech theater continues the age-old tradition of puppeteering.

There are many theaters around the Czech Republic that perform original plays, comedies, experimental works, and more traditional fare such as Shakespeare. Black Light theaters have popped up all over the Czech Republic. Like the luminescent puppet theaters, these performances take place under black lights. Dancers, actors, and special effects create truly unique theatrical experiences.

Theaters need plays, and the Czech Republic has many fine playwrights. The country's most famous playwright is its former president, Václav Havel. Several of his plays have been translated into other languages and are performed around the world.

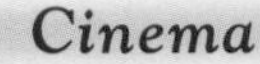

Cinema

The film industry stretches back to 1898 when the first silent films were being produced. Documentaries, newsreels, and dramas were all being made during the early years. Communists nationalized the film industry in the 1940s. They controlled the content of films, restricting artistic freedom. Writers and producers had more freedom making films with fictionalized stories using nonhuman characters. You could have puppets say and do things that humans might be imprisoned for saying. That's why puppet and cartoon films became so popular. Czech animated films achieved worldwide fame and continue to win major awards.

Czech filmmakers soared to new heights and international fame during the 1960s. The art movement at that time was called the Czech New Wave. Many Czech New Wave film directors have made films in America. Among the most successful is Milos Forman. Two of his films won Academy Awards: *One Flew Over the Cuckoo's Nest* and *Amadeus*, which

Festivals Galore

Czechs love their festivals. There are festivals throughout the year in cities and villages around the country. Types of festivals include those dedicated to film, music, wine, and beer.

Folklore festivals celebrate the unique costumes and customs from various regions. Each region has its own particular culture. Folk dancing, singing, music, and traditional foods are part of folk festivals. The largest and oldest folk festival is held yearly in Strážnice.

he shot in Prague. The Czech-made film *Kolya* won an Oscar award for best foreign film in 1997.

Though budgets are certainly well below Hollywood blockbuster films, Czech producers are well-respected worldwide. The country produces about thirty dramatic films each year.

Architecture

The Czech Republic is rich with elaborately built castles, cathedrals, monasteries, and public buildings. Prague in particular is a showcase of amazing architecture and is often referred to as the city of a hundred spires. Many of the sites and some whole towns have been designated as UNESCO World Heritage Sites. UNESCO is an acronym for the United Nations Educational, Scientific, and Cultural Organization. The main objective of this organization is to contribute to peace and security in the world by promoting collaboration among nations through education, science, culture, and communication. UNESCO helps preserve historically and culturally relevant sites through special funding. It also states that it is a violation of international law to destroy such sites.

Just as beautiful as the centuries-old cathedrals is the folk architecture found in many small villages. The folk architectural style was popular during the thirteenth century. Artists painted the outside of buildings and homes with pretty geometric designs and flower motifs. This kind of architecture has been well preserved in the south Bohemian village of Holašovice.

A beautiful street in Holašovice is a fine example of folk architecture.

Alphonse Mucha became famous for his posters of Sarah Bernhardt.

Painting and Fine Art

Among the early painters were those who adorned church walls with frescoes and murals of religious scenes. The Prague Academy of Art opened in 1796 and is where many Czech artists studied their craft. In the late nineteenth and early twentieth centuries, Czech painters were working in a style called Art Nouveau. The most famous Czech artist working during this period was Alphonse Mucha (1860–1939). He spent most of his early life in Paris. His most notable work was a series of posters featuring the actress Sarah Bernhardt. A Chicago businessman so appreciated his work that he sponsored Mucha to paint twenty large paintings depicting Slavic life. Mucha moved back to his homeland in 1922, where he continued to develop a variety of pieces such as stamps and banknotes. There is a museum dedicated to him in Prague.

Abstract painter František Kupka (1871–1957) created more abstract paintings using bright colors, geometric patterns, and also some with more flowing lines. His interest in spirituality and the occult was reflected in many of his paintings. His painting *Conqueror Worm* was inspired by an Edgar Allen Poe poem. Kupka was also a renowned book illustrator. He is considered among the finest abstract painters of his time. His paintings hang in museums around the world.

In the early twentieth century, cubism became the next wave of artistic style in Europe. Spanish artist Pablo Picasso is perhaps the best-known cubist. But there were many others who created paintings with disconnected geometric shapes including Czech painters. Famed sculptor Otto Guttfreund (1889–1927) worked in the cubist style but he later dropped it in favor of more realistic forms. He is considered among the greatest Czech sculptors.

***The Whirl* by František Kupka, a noted abstract painter.**

Decorated objects that can be used are called functional art. Ceramics, glassware, and furniture are examples of this kind of art, all of which are produced in the Czech Republic. The country, however, is best known as a producer of fine Bohemian crystal and glassware. Crystal is a type of glass that has some lead in it. It is the lead that makes the glass softer so that skilled artists can engrave patterns on it. Vases, drinking glasses, and chandeliers are all made from Bohemian crystal. Porcelain and ceramic items are also produced. Glassware mass-produced in factories is more common today but there are still many fine artists working with glass.

Museums Odd and Interesting

The Czech Republic has more than 700 museums. Some are typical, such as the those dedicated to literature, painting, and technology. Open-air museums showcase traditional village life in simple rural architectural buildings. One of the more odd museums is the Museum of Medieval Torture Instruments. The items displayed include thumbscrews, the head crusher, and the iron gag.

Life, Learning, and Leisurely Pursuits

Opposite: **Czechs love outdoor cafés like this one in Old Town Square, Prague.**

THE CZECH DAILY SCHEDULE BEGINS EARLY; MOST PEOPLE wake by 6 A.M. Factory workers and shopkeepers are at work by 7:00 A.M. And by 8 A.M., office workers are attending to business and students are in their classes. Lunch breaks are typically at noon. Many shops, especially those outside of Prague, close their doors at lunchtime. The business and school day ends between 5:00 and 7:00 P.M. and you'll find few shops open on the weekends. But life in the Czech Republic is certainly not all about work and no play! People have plenty of time for socializing, special interests, and diversions. For example, many people enjoy gardening. Even if they live in a city, they are likely to keep a small plot to grow some fruits and vegetables. Children and adults enjoy many different kinds of sports, and those who are interested in the arts have a variety of museums, cinemas, and theater performances to attend. The Czechs also love festivals. Throughout the summer in villages, towns, and cities you'll find festivals dedicated to everything from food, arts, and sporting interests.

Love for Learning

The Czech's love of learning extends back to the fourteenth century. King Charles IV built the first university in central Europe in 1348. Today there are twenty-three institutions of higher learning. The educational system is among the best in Europe.

Children hard at work in primary school.

The literacy rate is nearly 100 percent. Most Czechs speak two or three foreign languages. Kindergarten begins at the young age of three and lasts three years. From six to fifteen years of age children go to *základní skola* (basic school) where they receive a well-rounded general education. After completing their general studies they can choose a vocational school where they will learn a specific skill such as auto mechanics. Or students can attend a four-year university preparatory school, called gymnasium. Studies keep students busy, but not so much that they don't have time for some fun.

Sports

In 1862, a Czech university professor, Miroslav Tyrš, recognized that a healthy mind needed a healthy body. He developed the first Czech educational exercise program and based it on gymnastics. The program was called Sokol, which means falcon in Czech. Sokol was a group exercise for people of all ages. It was also highly patriotic. During Sokol festivals, participants wore traditional Czech costumes and rallied for independence. Because of its politics, Sokol was banned by the Germans and Communists. Today, however, the festivals have been revived and are celebrated around the country. There are even Sokol groups in other countries that have Czech communities. There are several Sokol groups in the United States.

This Sokol festival celebrates an important Czech tradition of sport and culture.

Rogaining: The Sport of Orienteering

A relative newcomer to the sports world in the Czech Republic is a sport that involves long distance cross-country orienteering. With a map and compass, teams must find their way through all kinds of terrain from farmlands to mountains. It's a natural obstacle course that must be navigated on foot.

The goal is to pass through as many checkpoints as possible within a predetermined time period. The more serious events are held over a 24-hour period and are regulated by the International Rogaining Federation. The Czech Republic was host to the fifth annual World Rogaining Championships in 2002. A Czech team came in a respectable second place.

There are, however, many different levels of this sport. Distances can vary from as little as 6 miles (10 km) to as many as 37 miles (60 km). The sport attracts everyone from grandparents to grandchildren. It's a fun way to spend a day outdoors.

Czechs turn to the great outdoors for a number of sporting interests. The mountains provide perfect places for hiking, skiing, rock climbing, and orienteering. In summer, the many lakes and rivers become popular places for windsurfing and water skiing. Weekend getaway trips to country cottages are common.

A cross-country skier enjoys the peaceful countryside.

Soccer, ice hockey, and tennis are especially popular sports in the Czech Republic. There are many local amateur sports associations for young and older enthusiasts. There are tennis courts in nearly every city, town, and village. The Czech Republic has produced some world-renowned tennis champions such as Martina Navrátilová and Ivan Lendl.

Professional Czech athletes have done well in international competitions. The Czechoslovak soccer team won the World Championships in 1934 and 1962. In 2002 the Czech National Hockey Team was ranked as the second best in the world. They won the World Hockcy Championships eight

The National hockey team celebrates success at the 2001 World Championship game.

Czech Tennis Champion

Martina Navrátilová, one of the best tennis players in world, was born in Prague in 1956. She won the semifinals during her first tournament when she was just eight years old. As a professional, Navrátilová dominated the women's professional tennis scene during the 1980s. Her achievements include 56 Grand Slam titles, 167 tournament wins in singles, 166 wins in doubles, and the Grand Slam of tennis in 1983–1984. She was inducted into the International Tennis Hall of Fame in 2000. Today, she continues to compete in select tournaments.

times and the Olympic gold medal in 1988. Among the most honored Olympic athlete was Vera Cásalvská. During her years as a competitive athlete (1960–1968), she won seven Olympic medals in gymnastics in addition to many medals in other competitions. In 1998 she was inducted into the International Gymnastics Hall of Fame.

Two Birthdays for Every Czech

Czechs celebrate special personal holidays called "name days." Every day in the year has a name. When the day for your name comes along, there's a celebration much like a birthday party. Your family and friends get together to share your favorite meal and to give you gifts.

Food and Drink

Czech cuisine is accented by culinary traditions from other countries such as Germany, Austria, and Hungary. Czechs add their own particular twists to other countries' traditions but by name alone you can figure out where some dishes originated. For example, there's goulash, a Hungarian stew, and Wiener schnitzel, a veal dish from Austria. The *knedlíky*, however, is an original Czech specialty. It is a dumpling served as a side dish with most meals, and can also be made into a sweet treat.

Soup is usually the first course served for dinner and also makes for a popular midday meal. There's quite a variety of Czech soups, they are made thick like a stew or thin like a broth. Traditional soups include garlic soup, which is light and easy to prepare. Thicker soups are generally made from meats and vegetables such as cabbage soup flavored with smoked meat and thickened with cream. There are also regional soup specialties. For example, in the foothills of the Giant (Krkonose) moŭntain range, cooks prepare a thick sour soup

Forest Fungus

Mushroom picking is a favorite national pastime in the Czech Republic. Many different kinds of mushrooms grow in the thick forests. Not just any old mushroom will do, however—many are poisonous. But expert mushroom collectors know well the difference between the edible and toxic variety. Wild mushrooms are most often enjoyed simply stir-fried with eggs. They are also used in soups and sauces.

made from cream, potatoes, eggs, and mushrooms topped off with the herb dill.

Meat is generally the main course, pork being the favorite. Roast pork loin seasoned with caraway seeds is typically served with dumplings and cabbage. Caraway seeds, in fact, are used in many meats and some vegetable dishes. Most Czechs would insist that pork meals are best washed down with a good Czech beer. Other meats enjoyed include lamb, usually made with roasted garlic, beef boiled or stewed, and roast goose or duck are favorite holiday meats. Game meats such as venison are considered Czech specialties.

Czechs love their deserts. Their famed dumplings appear on the sweets menu stuffed with fresh fruit or jam. The dumplings are sprinkled with powdered sugar, cinnamon, and sometimes with ground walnuts. Seasonal fruits such as apricots in summer

Cookies Fit for a President

Vanilla crescents are a Christmas tradition and a favorite of former president Václav Havel. The following recipe makes about thirty-six cookies

1 stick unsalted butter at room temperature
1/2 cup sugar
2 cups all-purpose white flour, sifted
1 1/4 cup ground almonds
1 tsp vanilla extract
confectioners sugar

Cream the butter and sugar together until light and fluffy. Blend in flour 1/2 cup at a time then add almonds and vanilla extract. Beat until the mixture becomes slightly stiff. Shape the dough into a ball, wrap in wax paper, and refrigerate for about an hour.

Preheat the oven to 350 degrees. Lightly oil two cookie sheets or use nonstick cookie sheets. Tear off tablespoon-sized chunks of the dough and place them on a floured working surface. Roll each one into a strip about 2 inches long and shape them into crescents. Place the crescents about 1/2 inch apart on baking sheet. Bake for 15–20 minutes until golden brown. Let cool for five minutes then dust with powdered sugar.

or blueberries in autumn make for an extra special dumpling filling. On the breakfast table is another Czech specialty, baked yeast buns. The buns are stuffed with a sweet cottage cheese, poppy seeds, or jam and are oven baked. They are topped off with a dusting of powdered sugar.

Most countries have some sort of pancake, and the Czech Republic is no exception. Their pancake is thin like the French crepe and is called *palačinky* (pah-la-CHIN-kee). These pancakes are served with many different kinds of sweets such as chocolate, fruit, or ice cream.

Fruit dumplings are popular sweet treats.

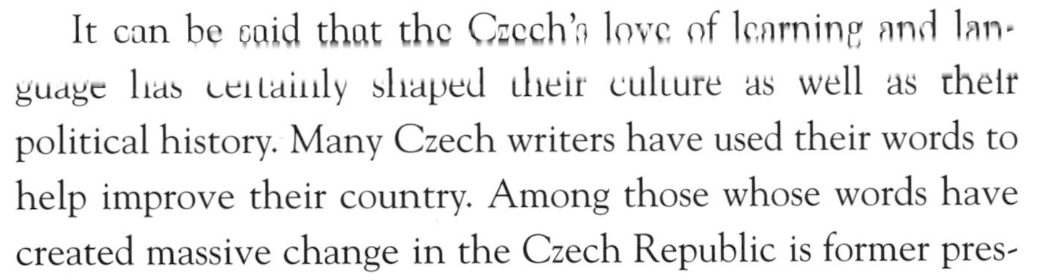

It can be said that the Czech's love of learning and language has certainly shaped their culture as well as their political history. Many Czech writers have used their words to help improve their country. Among those whose words have created massive change in the Czech Republic is former president Václav Havel. He is perhaps as well known for his clever theatrical plays as he is for his political diplomacy. He has said this about the power of words, "I really do inhabit a system in which words are capable of shaking the entire government structure, where words can prove mightier then ten military divisions." It is a belief that carries the Czech Republic with hope and optimism into the future.

National Holidays

New Years Day/Republic Day	January 1
Easter Monday	March or April
Labor Day	May 1
Liberation Day	May 8
Cyril and Methodius Day	July 5
Jan Hus Day	July 6
Saint Wenceslas Day	September 28
Czechoslovakian Statehood Day	October 28
Freedom and Democracy Day	November 17
Christmas Holidays	December 24 and 25

Timeline

Czech History			World History
		2500 B.C.	Egyptians build the Pyramids and the Sphinx in Giza.
		563 B.C.	The Buddha is born in India.
		A.D. 313	The Roman emperor Constantine recognizes Christianity.
Kingdom of Samo establishes first Slavic stronghold in Moravia.	600s	610	The Prophet Muhammad begins preaching a new religion called Islam.
Great Moravian Empire emerges. Establishment of the Bohemian Přemysl dynasty.	800s		
Collapse of Great Moravian Empire.	894		
		1054	The Eastern (Orthodox) and Western (Roman) Churches break apart.
		1066	William the Conqueror defeats the English in the Battle of Hastings.
		1095	Pope Urban II proclaims the First Crusade.
		1215	King John seals the Magna Carta.
		1300s	The Renaissance begins in Italy.
Collapse of Přemysl dynasty.	1306		
Luxembourg Dynasty, Bohemian King Charles IV rules.	1346		
		1347	The Black Death sweeps through Europe.
		1453	Ottoman Turks capture Constantinople, conquering the Byzantine Empire.
		1492	Columbus arrives in North America.
		1500s	The Reformation leads to the birth of Protestantism.
Habsburg (German) Dynasty takes possession of Czech lands.	1526		
Czech Republic uprising defeated by Habsburg at Battle of White Mountain.	1620		
		1776	The Declaration of Independence is signed.
		1789	The French Revolution begins.

Czech History

Habsburg Dynasty strikes deal with Austria-Hungary, forming Austro-Hungarian Empire.	1867
Austro-Hungarian Empire loses power.	1914
Allied nations recognize Czechoslovakia as an independent republic.	1918
Hitler and the Nazis annex Czechoslovakia.	1939
Soviet Union liberates Czechoslovakia from Nazis.	1945
Communist rule.	1948–1989
Prague Spring.	1968
Pivotal nonviolent protest in Prague. Václav Havel elected president.	1989
Czech Republic and Slovakia split, each becoming an independent country.	1993

World History

1865	The American Civil War ends.
1914	World War I breaks out.
1917	The Bolshevik Revolution brings communism to Russia.
1929	Worldwide economic depression begins.
1939	World War II begins, following the German invasion of Poland.
1945	World War II ends.
1957	The Vietnam War starts.
1969	Humans land on the moon.
1975	The Vietnam War ends.
1979	Soviet Union invades Afghanistan.
1983	Drought and famine in Africa.
1989	The Berlin Wall is torn down, as communism crumbles in Eastern Europe.
1991	Soviet Union breaks into separate states.
1992	Bill Clinton is elected U.S. president.
2000	George W. Bush is elected U.S. president.
2001	Terrorists attack World Trade Towers, New York, and the Pentagon, Washington, D.C.

Fast Facts

Official name: Czech Republic
Capital: Prague
Official language: Czech

Brno

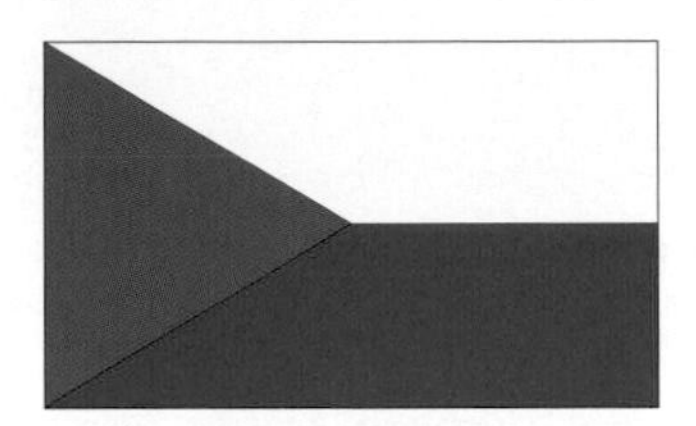

Country's flag

Krkonoše Mountain

Official religion: None

Year of founding: January 1, 1993, Independence Day

National anthem: "Kde domov muj?" "Where is my home?"

Type of government: Parliamentary democracy

Chief of state: President

Head of government: Prime minister

Geographic coordinates: 49° 45' N, 15° 30' E

Area: The Czech Republic is 30,450 square miles (78,864 sq km)

Bordering countries: Austria, Germany, Poland, Slovakia

Highest and lowest elevation: Highest point: Sněžka mountaintop, 5,256 feet (1,602 m)
Lowest point: Labe (Elbe) River, 384 feet (117 m)

Average temperatures: Prague, January, 27°F (–3°C), July, 64°F (18°C); Brno, January, 29°F (–2°C), July, 67°F (19°C)

Average precipitation: Prague: 18.8 inches (477 mm)
Brno: 19.6 inches (497 mm)

National population: 10,256,760 (2002 est.)

Population of largest cities:

Prague	1.2 million
Brno	388,596
Ostrava	325,827
Pilsen (Plzeň)	171,908
Olomouc	105,862

Charles Bridge

Currency

Famous landmarks:

- ***Charles Bridge,*** Prague
- ***Prague Castle,*** Prague
- ***The Old Town Hall with astrological clock,*** Prague
- ***Gothic Cathedral of Saint Barbara,*** Kutná Hora
- ***Sandstone labyrinths,*** Kokořín
- ***Church of Saint Bartholomew,*** Pilzen

Industry: Forty-one percent of the country's labor force is employed in manufacturing. Czech factories process raw materials and make finished products. Some factories process iron, steel, and other metals. Other factories construct large machines that make such items as shoes and wood products. These automated machines are exported to other countries around the world. Czechs make many finished products including transportation vehicles, machines and tools, chemicals, electronics, glass, jewelry, beer, foods, and pharmaceuticals.

Currency: The basic units of currency are the heller and the koruna, meaning crown. There are 100 hellers in one koruna. One U.S. dollar is worth approximately 30 korunas.

System of weights and measures: Metric system

Literacy rate: 99.9%

Czech child

Václav Havel

Common words and phrases:

Prosim	Please
Dekuji	Thank you
Ano	Yes
Ne	No
Ja	I
Matka	Mother
Otec	Father
Anglicky	English
Dobry den	Good Day
Na shledanou	Goodbye
Nerozumím.	I do not understand.
Jak se máte?	How are you?

Famous Czechs:

Antonín Dvořák (1841–1904)
Classical music composer

Milos Forman (1932–)
Film director

Václav Havel (1936–)
Dramatist, and former president of the Czech Republic

Franz Kafka (1883–1924)
Writer

Milan Kundera (1929–)
Writer

Alphonse Mucha (1860–1939)
Artist/painter

Martina Navrátilová (1956–)
Tennis player

Bedřich Smetana (1824–1884)
Opera composer

To Find Out More

Books

- Martin, Pat. *Czechoslovak Culture: Recipes, History, and Folk Arts*. Iowa City: Penfield Press, 1989.
- Nollen, Tim. *Culture Shock*. Portland, Oregon: Graphic Arts Center Publishing Company, 1997.
- Sioras, Efstathia. *Cultures of the World: Czech Republic*. Tarrytown, New York: Marshall Cavendish, 1999.

Video

- *Czech Republic and Southern Poland*. Lonely Planet Publications, 1999.

Web Sites

- **The World Factbook**
  http://www.cia.gov/cia/publications/factbook/
  The CIA site has frequently updated stats and summaries of geography, history, economy, and more.

- **Embassy of the Czech Republic**
  http://www.mzv.cz/washington/
  The Czech Republic Embassy in Washington, D.C., hosts a site that includes detailed information on economy, trade, and links to other Czech government sites.

- **The Czech National Museum**
  http://www.nm.cz/english
  This site has details about Czech art history, architecture, and information on the museum's collection.

- **Current Affairs**
  http://www.radio.cz/en/
  The site of Radio Prague, which covers a variety of subjects such as Czech music, government affairs, and science.

Index

Page numbers in *italics* indicate illustrations.

Meet the Author

JoAnn Milivojevic is a freelance writer and video producer who loves to travel and explore. During her youth, she wandered along creeks and railroad tracks inspecting plants and creatures. By traveling a straight line, she could get fully absorbed in her explorations and would always be able to find the way back home. Today, her wanderings are more global. She explores cities, villages, forests, and oceans, and occasionally gets lost in the process. Fortunately, she has found that people are generally kind and eager to help her, even though she can't always speak their language.

To research the Czech Republic she traveled mostly via the Internet, and to Chicago-area libraries, bookstores, and art galleries. She read Czech English-language newspapers, listened to Czech music, watched travel videos, sampled Pilsner Urquell beer, and baked a batch of Czech vanilla crescent cookies just to get the proper taste of things.

In articles written about the Czech Republic, she discovered today's Czech youth have what America's young have, such as a wealth of magazines, Internet access, video games, and even American fast food restaurants. Their parents, on the other hand, weren't so lucky—they were excited when someone traveled and brought back common items like herbal-scented shampoo.

In addition to writing cultural geography books, JoAnn writes about fitness, food, and travel for magazines and newspapers nationwide. Her love of exploration has taken her on hikes in Trinidad rainforests, scuba diving in the Cayman Islands, and mountain biking in Utah. This is her third book for Children's Press.

Photo Credits

Photographs © 2004:

A Perfect Exposure/Lubomir Stiburek: 18, 23, 121
AKG-Images, London: 116 (Erich Lessing), 47 (Musee de Louvre, Paris), 97 (Private Collection), 43, 49, 56 bottom, 75, 96, 108, 111
AP/Wide World Photos: 64 top (Kerim Okten), 64 bottom (Tomas Turek), 36
Art Resource, NY/Scala: 117
Brown Brothers: 50 top
Corbis Images: 45 (Archivo Iconografico, S.A.), 30 (Andre Burian), 124 (Duomo), 118 (Dave G. Houser), 11, 87, 88, 92, 132 bottom (Barry Lewis), 85 (Jose F. Poblete), 123 (Reuters NewMedia Inc.), 72 (Shepard Sherbell), 33 top (Richard Hamilton Smith), 40 (David Turnley), 109 (Adam Woolfitt)
Corbis SABA: 70 (Peter Blakely), 67 (Leif Skoogfors)
Corbis Sygma/David Brauchli: 94
Getty Images/Sean Gallup: 27, 122
Hulton | Archive/Getty Images: 52
Network Aspen /Jeffrey Aaronson: 79
North Wind Picture Archives: 48
Panos Pictures: 60, 91 (Heidi Bradner), 81 top (Liba Taylor), 12 (Gregory Wrona)
Peter Arnold Inc.: 58 (FOVA/Sagl-Jiranek), cover, 2, 6, 7 bottom, 17, 21, 24, 26, 28, 32 top, 39 bottom, 69 right, 82, 99, 102, 104, 106, 130, 131, 132 top (Oldrich Karasek), 107 (Helga Lade)
Photo Researchers, NY: 39 top (St. Meyers/Okapia), 38 top (Elisabeth Weiland), 38 bottom (Terry Whittaker)
Sovfoto/Eastfoto/CTK: 37 (Jan Cerny), 90 bottom (Michal Krumphanzl), 127 (Dan Krzywon), 74 (Tomas Novak), 77 (Ballon Mierny Otto), 20, 115 (Jaroslav Sybek), 33 bottom, 35 (Galgonek Vladislav), 78 (Libro Zavoral), 9, 16, 19, 32 bottom, 44, 46, 50 bottom, 56 top, 57, 63, 66, 76, 81 bottom, 103, 108 bottom, 112, 113, 120, 125, 133 bottom, 133 top
Superstock, Inc.: 14, 100 (Profimedia), 22 (Kurt Scholz), 7 top, 25
The Image Works: 34 bottom (Eastcott/Momatiuk), 114 (Hideo Haga/HAGA)
Tim Thompson: 90 top
Transit Photo and Archive/Thomas HSrtrich/Sovfoto: 34 top
TRIP Photo Library: 8 (J Ellard), 101 (N Price), 69 left (A Tovy)
Maps by XNR Productions Inc.